Praise for LOOK BEFORE YOU LIRP

"*The Power of Zero strategy is one that I have implemented both personally and with my clientele. If you are an advisor, your clients need this type of planning. It is not the rate of return but the after-tax income that is important. The LIRP is an excellent way to enhance an overall financial plan.*"

—DARCY BERGEN, CRFA, BERGEN FINANCIAL GROUP, MESA, AZ

"*If you're diligently saving for retirement, be sure to read* Look Before You LIRP. *David McKnight will challenge you to re-think the common assumption that you'll 'be in a lower bracket' when you retire. Then he'll show you what to do so that your retirement nest egg isn't vaporized by taxes. On second thought, don't read this book … study it!*"

—STEVE SAPPINGTON, TRINITY WEALTH MANAGEMENT, WACO, TX

"*David McKnight has done it again! In this follow-up to* The Power of Zero, *he makes a powerful case that all life insurance retirement plans are not, in fact, created equal. This book is a must-read if you plan on overcoming the obstacles that stand between you and the zero percent tax bracket. Bravo!*"

—LARRY DELEGGE, DELEGGE FINANCIAL, SCHAUMBURG, IL

"*David has provided a clear roadmap for getting from taxable and tax-deferred to tax-free over time. His is a balanced approach, one that our clients can comprehend and easily implement. As a financial professional I know that most financial advisors are not even having a conversation about this with their clients. This has been a key differentiator for us.*"

—JERRY IACANGELO, IACANGELO FINANCIAL GROUP, LLC, SHREWSBURY, NJ

"*The LIRP is largely misunderstood by both consumers and advisors. In this book, the author does an exceptional job of simplifying a complex subject. David McKnight is a man of integrity and a true leader in our industry.*"

—LANE MARTINSEN, RFC® RICP®, MARTINSEN GOLDBERG FINANCIAL GROUP, SCOTTSDALE, AZ

"The 'Power of Zero' approach creates more spendable retirement income than any other financial planning strategy I have seen. And, as this book demonstrates, the LIRP is the 'Swiss Army Knife' of financial tools and an important part of the zero-tax approach. No other financial tool has the versatility to accomplish so much."

—DON CAMERON, CLU, RICP, CAMERON FINANCIAL SERVICES, FISHERS, IN

"The LIRP is one of the most powerful and versatile planning tools available. This book gives valuable insight on how to find the right LIRP with the right company."

—DAVID HANCOCK, LUTCF, DAVID HANCOCK FINANCIAL, GREENVILLE, AL

"David McKnight's two books, The Power of Zero *and* Look Before You LIRP, *have laid the foundation for the future of retirement income planning and are impacting the entire industry's view on tax strategy in retirement. Truly a game-changer!"*

—JORDAN D. MAIN, CPA, MBA, MAIN FINANCIAL GROUP, BRIGHTON, MI

"David McKnight's tax-free strategies have opened my eyes to the reality that nearly all of my clients can have a tax-free retirement. As this book explains, using the right LIRP can help protect against higher taxes, market crashes, and long term care expenses."

—JARED L. DAVIS, CFP®, DAVIS WEALTH MANAGEMENT, BOISE, ID

"Important, worthwhile and easy to understand. Look Before You LIRP *by David McKnight is a must read for anyone planning for retirement."*

—DAWN HARKINS, DAWN K. HARKINS, LLC, SLIDELL, LA

"Like its predecessor The Power of Zero, Look Before You LIRP *has revolutionized my financial planning practice. This book dispels the most common myths about life insurance retirement plans and shows you how to find the right one for your tax-free retirement strategy."*

—RICK STEVENS, STEVENS FINANCIAL GROUP, MACON, GA

"The concepts taught by David are powerful strategies that most Americans can benefit from. His first book is already a 'must read' for my tax clients, and this book will now be added to that list."

—KORY A. HOLKER, ATA, ASSET PROTECTION SERVICES, INC., MINNEAPOLIS, MN

"McKnight has demystified the LIRP and written a clear guide to finding the most suitable combination of features for an effective LIRP strategy. Written in an accessible, conversational style, this book can be easily understood by the client, and even the most seasoned professional will learn new things. I know I did."

—CONRAD KUNKEL, MLIR, GPS STRATEGIES, LLC, CHAPEL HILL, NC

"As a follow up book to The Power of Zero, Look Before you LIRP *is an outstanding resource for financial professionals as well as consumers on understanding the differences in life insurance retirement plans and which plans work best for tax-free income. Thank you David, for writing this book!"*

—DAVID PARKER, RETIREMENT PLAN CONSULTANTS, LLC, TUPELO, MS

"David's first book The Power of Zero *might very well be the most transformational financial message of our time for both clients and their advisors. In this second book, David delves deeper into the appropriate application of that message with truth and candor that cannot be ignored!"*

—DARRYL R. WILSON, PROVIDENT PLANNING, LLC, BIRMINGHAM, AL

"Like in The Power of Zero, *David takes a very complex subject matter and breaks it down into an understandable read. Anyone reading* Look Before You LIRP *will come away with a new appreciation for the power of a properly selected and designed LIRP as part of a tax-free retirement plan."*

—MIKE RAITT, CPA, THE ALMEGA GROUP, PLANO, TX

*"*Look Before You LIRP *helps define the ideal LIRP in a way that is easy to read and understand. Anyone planning on utilizing the LIRP as part of a balanced approach to tax-free retirement planning should learn the information and strategies laid out in this book. Thanks David!"*

—MICHAEL SNOWHITE, CRFA, CALIFORNIA EDUCATORS, WOODLAND HILLS, CA

"In Look Before You LIRP, *David McKnight shows how to maximize the effectiveness of the LIRP as part of a well-balanced approach to tax-free retirement. Thank you David!"*

—SHAWN DAVENPORT, FORESIGHT FINANCIAL, ROSWELL, GA

"This powerful, practical book shows you how the right LIRP can be a critical part of your tax-free retirement roadmap. It's a must read for both consumers and their advisors."

—JASON FOSTER, GLOBALONE ADVISORS, INC., CORONA, CA

"For the average consumer, buying a life insurance retirement plan before reading this book is like getting married via a prearranged marriage. If you want to get married to the right LIRP, this book will show you how."

—MATT BURKLUND, INVESTMENT ADVISOR REPRESENTATIVE (IAR), RENTON, WA

"The LIRP is one of the most foundational, powerful, yet misunderstood strategies in the tax-free arsenal. That being said, all LIRPs are not created equal. Look Before You LIRP *is a must read for anyone who plans on making the LIRP a part of their tax-free retirement strategy."*

—BRIAN HANSON, HANSON WEALTH MANAGEMENT, EDEN PRAIRIE, MN

"David McKnight's newest masterpiece, Look Before You LIRP, *is a straight forward step-by-step lesson on how to properly evaluate and choose the correct type of life insurance retirement plan as part of an overall tax-free retirement strategy."*

—BRIAN BRITT, CONCERT WEALTH MANAGEMENT, SAN DIEGO, CA

*"*Look Before You LIRP *provides a deeper dive in to the fundamentals of using the life insurance retirement plan as a piece of your retirement planning puzzle. In easy to understand terms, David shows what to look for and which questions to ask when considering a LIRP. Thank you Dave!"*

—CRAIG JERGENSON, CFP, COACH CRAIG FINANCIAL, MAPLE GROVE, MN

LOOK
BEFORE YOU
LIRP

Why All Life Insurance Retirement Plans
Are <u>Not</u> Created Equal, and
How to Find the Right One for You

David McKnight

For my children

ACKNOWLEDGMENTS

I'd like to begin by acknowledging the legions of financial advisors who read *The Power of Zero*, embraced the tax-free paradigm, and conveyed it to their clients. It was largely through their efforts that *The Power of Zero* reached critical mass. These same financial advisors are on the front lines tirelessly proclaiming the virtues of tax-free planning in a world where the tax-deferred paradigm still holds sway. Without their efforts many Americans would still be sitting on the train tracks bracing for the impact of higher taxes. Without their advocacy, there would have been no audience for this second book. To them, I give my wholehearted thanks.

To the dozens of financial advisors who served as a sounding board for this book, I also give thanks. Their insight, attention to detail, and passion for tax-free retirement planning infused this book with a sharpness and focus that helped bring its message home. For over two years these same advisors encouraged me to write this follow-up to *The Power of Zero*. They insisted that another book needed to be written to bring the Life Insurance Retirement Plan into sharper focus. Through their prodding, the vision for this book slowly materialized and ultimately came to fruition. In many ways, this book is theirs, and for their encouragement I am grateful.

To my editor Gordon Warnock, thank you for your guiding hand, your patience, and your willingness to work long hours to meet deadlines. Your outside-the-box thinking and flair helped give this book personality and verve. Your contributions helped turned this book into a worthy companion to *The Power of Zero*.

I do, of course, save the most important for last. I've been married to my beautiful wife Felice for 16 years, and she has been my rock and my lodestar. She is good and virtuous and inspires me to do better and be better. She brought seven amazing children into the world and does the often unheralded work of turning our house into a home. Without her tireless efforts and unfailing support none of this would have been possible. To her I pledge my undying love and devotion.

CONTENTS

CHAPTER ONE
FINDING THE RIGHT LIRP

If you read my bestselling book *The Power of Zero*, I hope you found the prospect of getting into the 0% tax bracket in retirement both exhilarating and achievable. I also hope that you came away from the book more cognizant of a few important and undeniable realities. First, taxes *are* going up. There's no way around it. Unfortunately, the only way to liquidate our nation's growing debt load and pay for unfunded obligations like Social Security and Medicare is to double taxes over time.[1] It's simple math. Second, the only way to truly insulate yourself from the impact of higher taxes is to get yourself into the 0% tax bracket. Why? Because if tax rates double, and you're in the 0% tax bracket, two times zero is still zero! Third, in many cases, it's impossible to get to the 0% tax bracket without using a Life Insurance Retirement Plan (LIRP). That's a key proposition, and it's the one driving this book.

For many of you, the LIRP was the one concept in *The Power of Zero* with which you were least familiar. Finding out more about the LIRP may even be what led you to this book! Well, the LIRP *is* a transformational tax-free retirement tool and it merits a full examination. If you're skeptical about using life insurance as a potential retirement tool, let me simply say this: *you don't have to love life insurance or even life insurance companies, you just have to like them a little bit more than*

---

[1] http://www.cnn.com/2009/POLITICS/04/15/walker.tax.debt/

you like the IRS. Because in the end, not utilizing the LIRP may actually keep you out of the 0% tax bracket, in which case, the IRS wins. How does the IRS win? Remember, if you can't get into the 0% tax bracket, the next best tax bracket isn't 1% or even 2%. It jumps all the way up to 10%. Throw in another 6% for state taxes and now you're looking at 16%. And, if the experts are right, and tax rates double, 16% is starting to look more like 32%. All of the sudden, barely missing the 0% tax bracket can end up costing you hundreds of thousands of dollars at a time in your life when you need the money the most. When it comes to tax brackets in retirement, you can't afford to settle for second place!

Given the crucial role the LIRP can play in propelling you into the 0% tax bracket, it's important that we review the qualities that make it such a powerful tax-free retirement planning tool:

1. **No Penalties Pre-59 ½:** Unlike retirement accounts like 401(k)s or IRAs, there is no 10% penalty if you take money out of your LIRP before you reach age 59 ½.

2. **No 1099s:** The money within your LIRP's accumulation account doesn't get taxed as it grows like a mutual fund or a CD. This alone can save you thousands of dollars in unnecessary taxes over the course of your retirement.

3. **Distributions Are Not Reportable Income:** Remember, if you take money out of your LIRP in the right way, it doesn't show up on the IRS's radar as reportable income. In short, distributions are tax-free! Furthermore, it doesn't count as provisional income which could otherwise cause your Social Security to be taxed.

4. **No Contribution Limits:** Unlike the Roth IRA, the LIRP has no contribution limits. The IRS only stipulates that the amount of your contributions be tied to your death benefit. I have clients that contribute $50 a month to their LIRPs, and I have clients that contribute $200,000 per year, and everywhere in between.

5. **No Income Limits:** The Roth IRA was always intended for main-street America, so if your modified adjusted gross income is greater

than $194,000 you can no longer contribute. No such rules apply to the LIRP. It should come as no surprise to learn that 85% of the CEOs of Fortune 500 companies utilize the LIRP as one of their primary retirement planning tools.

6. **No Legislative Risk:** Though the IRS changed the rules on the LIRP in 1982, 1984, and 1988, every time they did so they made sure that whoever already had the LIRP got to keep it *and* continue to put money into it under the old rules for the rest of their lives. This history of "grandfather clauses" bodes well for the continued protection of LIRPs from the risk of future legislative changes.

To the casual observer, the LIRP seems like the perfect wealth accumulation tool—the proverbial alignment of the stars. You may even be tempted to put *all* of your money into the LIRP. But before you dump your entire life savings into a LIRP, it's important to recognize that the LIRP is not a panacea. It's not a silver bullet. If you're looking for a silver bullet, there are warehouses full of books and countless online advertisements that claim to cure all your retirement ills. The LIRP is simply a tool, one of multiple tax-free alternatives (along with Roth IRAs, Roth 401(k)s, and Roth Conversions) that help contribute to you being in the 0% tax bracket in retirement. That notwithstanding, the LIRP *is* an important part of a sound, tax-free retirement strategy, so it's critical it be understood and properly implemented.

So, You're Getting Married!

While properly structured LIRPs can contribute to your getting into the 0% tax bracket in retirement, not all of them will do so with the same level of efficiency or effectiveness. In fact, I would make the case that choosing the right LIRP is a bit like choosing the right spouse.

Remember back when you were single, in the prime of your youth, and looking for that special someone? You may not want to admit it, but I'd venture to say you probably had a laundry list of qualities you were looking for in a life-long partner. That list may have looked a little like this:

Given the long-term, legally binding nature of marriage, you wanted to be sure that your potential spouse had the right stuff—the qualities that would contribute to a long, happy partnership. Due to the nature of the traits on your list, there's a good chance you didn't propose to your spouse on the first date. In most cases your courtship would have lasted months or even years! One of our Founding Fathers reminded us of the importance of doing our due diligence before taking the plunge:

"Keep your eyes wide open before marriage.
Half shut afterward."

–Benjamin Franklin

In other words, marriage is a long-term proposition with far-reaching implications and you want to make sure you're hitching yourself to the right wagon.

Chances are you know someone who got caught up in a whirlwind romance that led to a hasty marriage to the wrong person. Blinded by love, they failed to look before they leapt. They tied themselves up in a long-term legal commitment without in-depth knowledge of the qualities—good and bad—that the person was bringing into the marriage partnership. It was a bit like watching a train wreck in slow motion, wasn't it? These types of marriages almost always end badly.

A long time ago, I heard a wise man impart some sound courtship advice to a friend. He said, "Before you get married, you need to know everything you possibly can about your future spouse. You have to become a private investigator. Talk to their roommates, talk to their classmates, talk to their teachers, talk to their childhood friends. Get to know their families." If giving that counsel today, he would almost certainly have recommended spending some quality time on Google as well. Why ask all these questions? Why do all this digging? Why be so comprehensive and thorough? Because if your future spouse has skeletons in their closet, it's in your best interest to bring them into the light of day *before* making a decision you may grow to regret.

Just as marriage is a long-term proposition that should not be entered into blindly or haphazardly, so is the LIRP. In short, you must "look before you LIRP!" Some LIRPs, frankly, have stipulations and provisions that you need to know about before you consider signing on the dotted line. In many cases, the untrained eye is unable to tease these qualities out of the pages and pages of legalese that make up these types of contracts. In fact, most people don't come to realize the legal implications of these provisions until years down the road when they're faced with a painful and expensive policy "divorce."

To head all this off at the pass, you have to be able to ask the right questions and look for the right qualities. You have to be a detective. You can't "look before you LIRP" if you don't know exactly what you're looking for. Consider this book your guide. It will help you lay the groundwork for a strong and satisfying LIRP marriage that will stand the test of time.

To aid you in your LIRP "courtship," I've assembled a laundry list of qualities that you should insist upon having before "tying the knot." Keep in mind that when evaluating LIRPs, *good* is the enemy of *best*. When you settle for a *good* LIRP, you do so at the expense of not having the *best* LIRP. To get the *best* LIRP for your tax-free retirement plan, one with which you can happily spend a lifetime, there are a few things you need to check off your list. The most important ones are as follows:

1. **Safe and Productive Growth:** It's not enough for your LIRP to be safe. Remember, savings accounts are safe, but they're a horrible way to fund your retirement. Most of the money you're planning on spending in retirement *hasn't even been earned yet*! We're looking

for a LIRP that can guarantee against market loss while at the same time delivering enough growth to make your retirement dollars last a lifetime.

2. **Low Fees:** Whatever you pay to your life insurance company in fees comes with opportunity cost. Not only do you lose those fees, but you lose what they could have earned for you had you been able to keep them and invest them back into your LIRP. To get the productive growth we talked about in quality #1, it's paramount that your LIRP have low fees.

3. **Tax-Free and Cost-Free Distributions:** By definition, every LIRP allows you to take money out tax-free. But not every LIRP allows you to do so cost-free. In some cases, the expenses for taking money out of your LIRP can end up costing you more than the taxes the LIRP is saving you! To operate at optimal efficiency, the distributions from your LIRP must be both tax-free *and* cost-free.

4. **A Cost-Free Long-Term Care Rider:** A long-term care event is arguably the worst thing that could happen to you in retirement. In fact, you're better off dying than needing long-term care (at least from a financial perspective). So, consequently, *everybody* loves the idea of having long-term care insurance. However, *nobody* loves the idea of paying for something they hope they never have to use. The right LIRP gives you cost-free long-term care protection without the heartburn of being locked into a use-it-or-lose-it proposition.

Now that you have your list, you can start evaluating your LIRP candidates. By way of review, there are essentially three types of LIRPs on the market. The primary distinguishing characteristic of these LIRPs is the manner in which your money grows in the accumulation fund. Those three growth strategies are as follows:

1. **Insurance Company Investment Portfolio:** Your cash value grows within the general investment portfolio of the insurance company. With this option, the insurance company assumes 100% of the

risk. Because insurance companies are conservative by nature, these rates of return tend to be conservative as well.

2. **Stock Market:** You invest your money in mutual fund portfolios called sub-accounts. With this approach, you assume 100% of the risk, and your returns rise and fall with the fluctuations of the stock market.

3. **Index:** Your accumulation account is linked to the upward movement of a stock market index like the S&P 500. You participate in the growth of the index up to a cap, while the insurance company guarantees that you'll never do worse than zero.

To be fair, all three of these options have one or more of the four essential qualities that I've enumerated. All three LIRPs, in fact, *may* help get you into the 0% tax bracket in retirement. But there is only one LIRP that possesses all four of these essential qualities. There is only one LIRP that is *best* equipped to help you enjoy a tax-free retirement: the indexed-based LIRP. In our industry, it's known as Indexed Universal Life (IUL), and it can be a powerhouse in your retirement planning picture.

In Chapters 2 through 5 of this book, I will expound upon each of the four qualities for evaluating a LIRP and show you how each is crucial to a successful LIRP marriage. Then I'll demonstrate how the IUL has been designed and engineered to embody each one of those attributes. I'll also describe the sometimes devastating implications of going without them. In Chapter 6, we'll drill a little deeper and define exactly what you should be looking for in an IUL because, at the end of the day, not all IULs are created equal. Finally, in Chapter 7, I'll take a balanced look at all of the myths surrounding the IUL and help you separate fact from fiction.

So, what do you think? Are you ready to lay the groundwork for the ideal LIRP marriage? Well, turn the page, and let's get started!

Chapter 1: Questions to Consider

1. Why is it important to get to the 0% tax bracket in retirement?

2. What features make the LIRP a powerful retirement tool?

3. In what way is starting an LIRP like getting married?

4. What are the four indispensable qualities of an ideal LIRP marriage?

5. What are the three available growth strategies in LIRP planning?

CHAPTER TWO
SAFE AND PRODUCTIVE

What?! Safe *and* productive? There's an oxymoron if there ever was one. The mere suggestion of "safe and productive" seems to defy the very laws of the investment universe. When it comes to retirement savings, most of us oscillate between two equally daunting extremes. We yearn for safety because we fear losing money at a period in our lives when we can least afford to. Yet, we recognize that without the stock market's productivity, we risk running out of money before we die. How do you win when confronted with two such starkly contrasting alternatives? Is there a way to achieve the best of both worlds? Is there a way to have your cake and eat it too? In other words, is it actually possible to achieve both safe *and* productive?

As it turns out, not only is this possible, it's necessary if you plan on getting the most out of your LIRP. The ability to be both safe and productive is an indispensable trait that must occupy the very top spot on your LIRP laundry list. Of the three types of LIRPs I discussed in Chapter 1, the only one that allows for truly safe and productive growth is Indexed Universal Life. Here's how the IUL works: the companies that sponsor these programs allow you to participate in the upward movement of a stock market index (say the S&P 500) up to a certain cap (say 13%). That's the productive part of it. Should that index go down in any given year, they simply credit you a zero. That's the safe part of it.

To illustrate the power of safe and productive growth, let's take a look at three years of S&P 500 returns[2] starting in 2008. Do you remember how the S&P 500 did in 2008? In short, it's how just about everyone did in 2008. That was the year in which the wheels of the economy really started to come off. It was the single greatest financial crisis since the Great Depression. Life as we knew it had changed forever. In 2008 alone, the S&P 500 dove an astounding 38.49%! The chart below shows the S&P 500's rates of return from 2008 to 2010. Now, given a cap of 13% and floor of 0%, how might your IUL have fared during those three years?

Year	S&P 500	IUL
2008	-38.49%	?
2009	23.45%	?
2010	12.78%	?

Well, if the worst you can do in your IUL is zero, what would your IUL's rate of return have been during the disaster of 2008? You guessed it! Zero! In 2009, the S&P rebounded in dramatic fashion, garnering 23.45%. If the best your IUL can do is 13%, how would you have done? You got it! 13%. If in 2010, the index did 12.78%, what would your growth account have been credited that year? That's right, 12.78%. The chart below fills in the blanks, demonstrating the IUL's balance of safety and productivity during that 3-year time period.[3]

Year	S&P 500	IUL
2008	-38.49%	0%
2009	23.45%	13%
2010	12.78%	12.78%

[2] For illustrative purposes in this book, we will be showing the S&P 500 without dividends
[3] While this chart is not representative of how an IUL might perform over every 3-year period, it does highlight the positive effects of a 13% cap and a floor of 0% during a period of severe stock market volatility

But Isn't Safety Over-Rated?

The typical buy-and-hold investor might say, "Hey, isn't all this just a little over-blown? Sure the stock market gives us a few down years every now and then, but that just goes with the territory. Without risk, there's no reward!" Is this true? Is concern over market risk much ado about nothing?

Let's explore the financial implications of investing in an unprotected S&P 500 index fund during that same 3-year period, this time using real dollar amounts. If you began 2008 with $100,000 and lost 38.49%, where would that leave you at the end of year 1? You got it, $61,510! So, what rate of return would you have to get in 2009 just to get back to your starting point of $100,000? The knee-jerk reaction would be 38.49%, since that's what you lost. The problem is, you'd be getting 38.49% on a much smaller number. 38.49% growth on $61,510 would only get you up to $85,185. You'd actually need to get an astounding 63% growth in that second year just to get back to square one!

Therein lies the problem: as we saw, the S&P 500's rate of return in 2009 wasn't 63%—it was only 23.45%. As a result, even with that impressive rebound, your initial $100,000 investment was still deep in the red at $75,934. Even after another successful year—that 12.78% growth of 2010—you'd find that buy-and-hold stock market investing didn't even get you back to where you'd started. At $85,638, you're still clawing your way back to even. Now you're beginning to understand why there was so much wide-spread panic!

Contrast this buy-and-hold scenario with a safe *and* productive IUL strategy with a 0% floor and a 13% cap. The chart below compares the IUL's year-by-year returns to unprotected S&P 500 investing.[4]

---

[4] This comparison does not include the S&P 500's expense ratios or the IUL's insurance and administrative expenses and is for illustrative purposes only

Initial Investment = $100,000			
Year	ROR	S&P 500	IUL
2008	-38.49%	$61,510	$100,000
2009	23.45%	$75,934	$113,000
2010	12.78%	$85,638	$127,441

As you can see, by the end of that same 3-year period, the IUL is already $41,803 ahead! Now, of course, 3 years of history doesn't tell the whole story, but the larger point is this: it can be very difficult to recover from a big down year, even if that down year is followed by several years of steady and consistent growth.

Volatility: The LIRP's Achilles Heel

A willingness to accept volatility in your IRAs or 401(k)s is one thing, but it's quite another when it comes to your LIRP. LIRPs have a potential Achilles heel when it comes to huge dips in the stock market, especially when those dips happen during your retirement years. To illustrate this for you, let's go back to a little Life Insurance 101. Let's build the intellectual case for why it's absolutely imperative that your LIRP have guarantees against market loss.

There's a basic formula that governs the relationship between your cash value, the amount of life insurance you're actually paying for in a given year, and your total death benefit. Understanding the relationship between these three variables will help illustrate why a 0% floor is indispensable. That formula is as follows:

$$\text{Cash Value} + \text{Life Insurance} = \text{Total Death Benefit}^{[5]}$$

---

[5] In life insurance industry terminology, this is known as death benefit option 1 or A. It's also known as a level death benefit

The following chart helps illustrate the interplay of these three variables:

Year	Cash Value	Life Insurance	Death Benefit
1	0	$500,000	$500,000
10	$100,000	$400,000	$500,000
20	$250,000	$250,000	$500,000

Notice how in year one (before you even make your first contribution), your cash value is at zero. At that point in the policy's life, you're paying for a full $500,000 of life insurance. Add the zero cash value to the $500,000 of life insurance and that gives you your total death benefit of $500,000. Thus:

$$\$0 + \$500,000 = \$500,000$$

But watch what happens when your cash value begins to grow. By year 10, your cash value is $100,000, which lowers the total amount of life insurance you're paying for that year to $400,000. Based on our formula, it would look like this:

$$\$100,000 + \$400,000 = \$500,000$$

By the time the cash value reaches $250,000 in year 20, you're only paying for $250,000 of life insurance. When we plug these numbers into our formula, this is what we get:

$$\$250,000 + \$250,000 = \$500,000$$

Some will lament the slow reduction of the life insurance portion (in this example $500,000 to $400,000 to $250,000) over the life or the policy, but this is actually a blessing in disguise. Here's why: the older you get, the more you pay for the cost of life insurance. However, when your cash value goes up, the amount of life insurance the IRS requires you to pay for (based on our formula) goes down. Because of this, the internal costs in your policy will actually stay level or even go down as time wears on. This allows your cash value to grow and compound even more productively!

But what happens if your LIRP's accumulation account is tied to the stock market with no down-side protection? Look to the formula. Two things can possibly happen in this situation, and neither one bodes well for the long-term viability of your LIRP:

1. **Market Loss**: If the market goes down 38.49% like it did in 2008, your stock market-based LIRP's cash value goes down right along with it. This can be challenging, especially if the drop happens during a period in your retirement when you were planning on drawing income from your LIRP.

2. **Increased Insurance Expenses**: When your cash value goes down in a stock market-based LIRP, the amount of insurance you're paying for actually goes up!

Of these two potential downfalls, the most devastating may be #2: Increased Insurance Expenses. To illustrate, let's modify the previous chart to reflect the volatility that comes with tying your LIRP to the stock market without protection. If, in year 21, we experienced a 20% drop in the stock market, we'd be looking at the following:

Year	Cash Value	Life Insurance	Death Benefit
1	0	$500,000	$500,000
10	$100,000	$400,000	$500,000
20	$250,000	$250,000	$500,000
21	$200,000	$300,000	$500,000

Notice that, in year 21 your cash value goes down by 20% requiring you to suddenly have to pay for an additional $50,000 of life insurance. Now, if the amount of insurance you're required to pay for goes up by $50,000, what do you suppose happens to your cash value? It's goes down again! Why? Because the cost of insurance comes out of your cash value. Paying for an extra $50,000 of life insurance may not seem like a big deal, but if that extra expense comes during a period of your life when your insurance expenses are high (in retirement, when you're older), this could deal a huge blow to your LIRP! But the damage doesn't stop there. Remember, if your insurance expenses go up, your cash value goes down. And if your cash value goes down again, what happens to your insurance expenses? They go up again! Talk about a death spiral! I've seen instances where this vicious cycle completely consumed a stock market-based LIRP's accumulation account leaving the policy holder emptyhanded, with no cash value *and* no death benefit! You can see how stock market losses can be a major Achilles heel for LIRPs that don't have down-side protection!

But don't panic! These types of seemingly hopeless scenarios are precisely where the IUL earns its keep. Instead of having to participate in the downturn of the stock market in a given year, the IUL simply credits you a zero, and it's effectively as if that year of losses didn't count. With that protection, the plummeting-cash-value-rising-insurance-expense scenario never comes into play. So, not only does the IUL safeguard you against market fluctuations, it protects you from a snowballing insurance expense nightmare that could sink your LIRP precisely at a time in your life when you need it the very most—during retirement.

So, now you see why it's absolutely imperative that we grow your LIRP accumulation account in a safe environment. Now we'll make the case for why your LIRP must have consistent, *productive* growth.

What Exactly Do You Mean by Productive?

I agree, "productive" can be a nebulous term, so let's be sure to define it for our purposes. Before doing so, however, let's harken back to an important concept from *The Power of Zero*. In that book we saw that in order to get to the 0% tax bracket, you have to have the perfect amount of money in each of your three buckets: taxable, tax-deferred and tax-free. If you have more than the ideal amount in either of the first two buckets, that surplus needs to be systematically repositioned into your tax-free bucket. In many cases, it makes sense to peel off a portion of that yearly shift, and direct it to your LIRP.

15

Now that we've laid some groundwork, let's work on crystallizing our definition of productive. Let's say that your shifting strategy calls for you to withdraw $10,000 per year from an IRA that's earning 7.5% and shift it to your LIRP. For the math to add up, you should expect to achieve similar performance from these dollars in the LIRP. In other words, if you can't duplicate the IRA's 7.5% growth in your LIRP, you risk offsetting the tax benefits that justify the LIRP's existence in the first place. For example, if your tax-free LIRP grows at only 5% over time, you risk running out of money much faster than if you'd simply left your money in your tax-deferred IRA that's earning 7.5%. In short, the LIRP has to be able duplicate what you were making in the original account or we can't mathematically justify the shift. That's what we mean by productive.

How Companies Accomplish Safe and Productive

One of the most common questions I get is, "How can life insurance companies possibly provide safe and productive growth?" Life insurance companies pull off the seemingly impossible by utilizing a strategy that incorporates both bonds and options. While most people are familiar with how bonds work, options can prove to be a bit more complicated. The following example, may help shed some light on the situation:

Let's say that you and I agree that your house has a market value of $300,000. I do want to buy your house, but not today. What I really want is the option to buy your house any time during the next year for $300,000. If you agree to that deal, I'll pay you $10,000 today. Ten months go by, and there's a big jump in the real estate market. Suddenly, that same house is worth $400,000. I then knock on your door and say, "Remember me and that agreement we signed?" At that point, I exercise my option to buy your house for $300,000, even though it's now worth $400,000. All told, I've spent

$10,000 on the option, and $300,000 on the house for a total of $310,000. I then sell the house for $400,000 and enjoy a $90,000 gain, all the while having risked only $10,000.

Now, were the house to decrease in value to $200,000 over the course of that year, I would simply let the option expire and walk away having only lost the $10,000 price of the option.

So, now that we know how options work, let's discuss how they operate in tandem with bonds to give us safe *and* productive growth. Let's say you make an annual contribution of $10,000 to your IUL. The insurance company takes your $10,000 and they subtract the cost of an option (say $500) on a stock market index, typically the S&P 500. They then invest your remaining $9,500 in a bond that earns enough over the course of a year's time to get you back to $10,000 (in this case the bond would need to grow 5.5%). So, at the end of one year's time, your $9,500 investment is once again worth $10,000. By utilizing this bond strategy companies can pay for the cost of the option while at the same time guaranteeing against market loss.

So that explains safe. But how about productive? Remember that option the insurance company bought for $500? That option allows you to participate in the growth of that S&P 500 index up to a cap—in this case we'll say 13%. If the index goes up 20%, you keep the first 13%. If it goes up 10%, you capture the full 10%. If the index goes down 20%, the company simply lets the option expire unexercised. No harm, no foul. And that, in a nutshell, is how insurance companies accomplish both safe and productive.

But, Do IUL's *Really* Have a Track Record of Being Productive?

At this point you're probably thinking to yourself, *Safe and productive sounds great, but can the IUL really grow as productively as my 401(k)?*

Fortunately IULs have been around since about the year 2000, so we have a full 15 years to gauge their productivity. As you may well know, during that time period the stock market has been nothing short of a roller coaster ride. That notwithstanding, some well-regarded IULs have actual, verifiable rates of return that may surprise you. Consider the following example of an IUL with a 14% cap and a floor of 0%.[6] Compare its rate of return to the S&P 500 over that same 15 year period:

Year	S&P 500 Returns	S&P 500 $1,000,000	IUL $1,000,000	Floor: 0% Cap: 14%
2001	-13.04%	$869,600	$1,000,000	0.00%
2002	-23.37%	$666,374	$1,000,000	0.00%
2003	26.38%	$842,163	$1,140,000	14.00%
2004	8.99%	$917,873	$1,242,486	8.99%
2005	3.00%	$945,409	$1,279,760	3.00%
2006	13.62%	$1,074,173	$1,454,063	13.62%
2007	3.53%	$1,112,091	$1,505,391	3.53%
2008	-38.49%	$684,047	$1,505,391	0.00%
2009	23.45%	$844,456	$1,716,145	14.00%
2010	12.78%	$952,377	$1,935,468	12.78%
2011	0.00%	$952,377	$1,935,468	0.00%
2012	13.41%	$1,080,090	$2,195,014	13.41%
2013	29.60%	$1,399,796	$2,502,315	14.00%
2014	11.39%	$1,559,232	$2,787,328	11.39%
2015	-0.73%	$1,547,849	$2,787,328	0.00%
	ROR	2.95%	7.07%	

[6] This comparison does not include the S&P 500's expense ratios or the IUL's insurance and administrative expenses and is for illustrative purposes only

[7] For illustrative purposes, we will be showing the S&P 500 without dividends

As you can see, it really pays to protect yourself from market downturns, even if you have to limit your potential upside in the process. In this example, your IUL's rate of return over that 15-year period was more than 4% higher, resulting in an additional $1.2 million dollars in growth. Safe and productive isn't just a nice slogan and it certainly isn't a pipe dream. It's actually achievable!

For those who are not satisfied with the IUL's *actual* 15-year track record, insurance companies often provide historical back testing. In other words, had the IUL been around for the last 20, 25, 30 or 40 years, how might it have fared? While historical back-testing is never a predictor of future results, it does give us some sense for how we might expect an IUL to perform moving forward. Leading IUL companies have consistently shown through back-testing that IULs, given today's variables, would have grossed at least 7.5% for each of the above-listed time periods.[8] In other words, the 15-year period we explored in our chart isn't merely a flash in the pan. It suggests that a program that allows you to participate in the upside of the market up to a cap while guaranteeing against market loss can be a sustainable, long-term wealth building strategy.

Some LIRPs promise safety but fail to deliver productive, stock market-like returns. This can be problematic if you plan on shifting money out of your 401(k) or IRA into your LIRP and hope to achieve similar rates of return. Other LIRPs make no guarantees on safety, but they allow you to participate in the full upside of the stock market. While participating in 100% of the market's gains can be seductive, in doing so, you also expose yourself to 100% of the market's downturns as well as the possibility of a snowballing insurance expense scenario that could bankrupt your LIRP. To maximize the effectiveness of your LIRP while minimizing the pitfalls along the way, you have to choose a LIRP that allows for both safe *and* productive growth. The only LIRP that has this indispensable quality is Indexed Universal Life.

---

[8] For each test a cap of at least 14% was utilized

Chapter 2: Questions to Consider

1. In what two ways is market volatility an Achilles heel for LIRPs?

2. What is the relationship between cash value and life insurance in the LIRP?

3. How does a LIRP perform differently than an IRA or 401(k) in a down market?

4. How do insurance companies accomplish "safe and productive?"

CHAPTER THREE
Low Fees

The second quality that should loom largely on your LIRP laundry list is low fees. After all, it doesn't matter how safe and productive your LIRP's growth is if, at the end of the day, you give it all away in fees! Remember, whatever you give back to the insurance company in the form of fees, is lost and gone forever. What's worse, you not only lose the fees, but you lose the opportunity cost on them as well. Opportunity cost represents what those fees could have earned for you had you been able to keep them and continue to invest them within your tax-free LIRP for the rest of your life. So, the greater the expenses, the less you get to spend in retirement! The success of your tax-free retirement strategy may depend, in large part, on your ability to find an LIRP that has low average annual expenses.

How Low is "Low"?

This, of course, begs the question: How do you define "low fees" when it comes to the LIRP? The fees associated with a LIRP can be very hard to quantify, so it's best to stick to the following guideline: your LIRP needs to have *average* yearly expenses that are as low as the tax-free alternative you might have utilized had the LIRP never been an option in the first place. For example, if you are funding your LIRP from money you might otherwise have converted to a Roth IRA, the cumulative, life-time fees in your LIRP need to be at least as low as the cumulative, life-time fees of your Roth IRA, assuming equal contributions. If your LIRP's fees are higher, then you risk neutralizing the tax benefits that justified using the LIRP in the first place. You see, your LIRP's fees have a direct bearing on its rates of return. If you have high rates of return *and* high fees, your LIRP will lose much of the mathematical justification for its existence. If you have low fees *and* high rates of return on the other hand, then ring those wedding bells because you've found the perfect recipe for matrimonial bliss. The right IUL, when structured properly, can strike that perfect balance.

A Tale of the Tape

Comparing an IUL's fees to those of tax-free alternatives like the Roth IRA, however, can be a tricky proposition, especially if you fixate on first-year expenses alone. Let's take a look at an example. The average expense ratio of a mutual fund is about 1.5% per year.[9] So, if you convert $10,000 to a Roth IRA, you can expect first year expenses of around $150. Conversely, if you redirect that $10,000 to a *properly structured* IUL, your average first year expenses might be closer to $1,500.

Expense Ratio

A measure of what it costs an investment company to operate a mutual fund. An expense ratio is determined through an annual calculation, where a fund's operating expenses are divided by the average dollar value of its assets under management. Operating expenses are taken out of a fund's assets and lower the return to a fund's investors.[10]

---

[9] http://www.fool.com/school/mutualfunds/costs/ratios.htm
[10] Investopedia.com

Based on this first-year comparison alone, it looks like the LIRP's fees are going to be *ten times* greater than the 1.5% minimum that we needed to justify its implementation. But, comparing first-year account balances hardly tells the whole story. Here's why: the fees associated with the Roth IRA are low when measured as a percentage of the first year's balance (in our example, 1.5% per year), but when measured in actual dollars over the life of the investment, the story changes dramatically. For example, if that $10,000 Roth IRA grew to $100,000, the annual fees would jump from $150 to $1,500. If it then grew to $1,000,000, the annual fees would balloon to $15,000. In other words, the more your Roth IRA grows, the more fees you pay.

Contrast that with the ongoing fees of a properly structured IUL. Generally speaking, when an IUL is set up to maximize the cash accumulation within the growth account, the fees stay relatively level. This is accomplished by buying as little life insurance as the IRS requires while stuffing as much money into it as the IRS allows. When you do this you maximize the benefits from the formula that governs the relationship between your cash value and the amount of life insurance you pay for in a given year. As we discussed in Chapter 2, that formula is as follows:

Cash Value + Life Insurance = Death Benefit

When your IUL has low fees, the lion's share of your contributions remain inside your tax-free growth account and continue to grow and compound over time. And, the more your money compounds, the less life insurance you have to pay for. The following chart shows how the amount of life insurance being paid for can reduce as the cash value grows over the policy holder's lifespan:

Age	Year	Cash Value	Life Insurance	Death Benefit
50	1	0	$500,000	$500,000
60	10	$100,000	$400,000	$500,000
70	20	$250,000	$250,000	$500,000
80	30	$400,000	$100,000	$500,000

As you can see, by the time the insured reaches 80 years old, he's only required to pay for $100,000 of life insurance! Can you imagine what would happen to this person's cash value were they required to pay for the full $500,000 of life insurance at this point in their life? Here's the point: even though the internal cost of life insurance in a properly structured IUL goes up as you age, the IRS requires you to buy less of it. This helps keep the IUL's fees relatively stable over the life of the program and saves you from getting slammed in the wallet as you advance in age.

Even though the fees in the IUL stay relatively level, they in fact grow *smaller* over time when calculated as a percentage of the overall cash value. For example, when an IUL's cash value grows from $10,000 to $100,000, that same $1,500 fee now represents only 1.5% of the total account value—the same as the Roth IRA. When the cash value of the IUL reaches $1,000,000, however, that $1,500 now represents only 0.15% of the cash value. The following chart demonstrates the IUL's cost-effectiveness over time when compared to the Roth IRA:

Roth	Account value	10,000	100,000	1,000,000
	Fee as % of balance	1.50%	1.50%	1.50%
	Fee as $ amount	$150	$1,500	$15,000
IUL	Cash value	10,000	100,000	1,000,000
	Fee as % of balance	15%	1.50%	0.15%
	Fee as $ amount	$1,500	$1,500	$1,500

What you'll find is that a low-fee IUL has average annual expenses at least as low as its tax-free counterpart, the Roth IRA. Granted, those expenses will be higher in the early years and lower in the later years, but when averaged out over the life of the program, they compare quite favorably with the tax-free alternatives that might otherwise have received that contribution.

Show Me the Math!

So how can we be certain that a properly structured IUL has low average annual expenses? We can find out by doing a side-by-side comparison between the IUL and a tax-free alternative such as the Roth IRA.[11] We begin by making equal contributions to both alternatives over a fixed period of time (say 10 years).[12] We also grow both accounts at a gross rate of 7.5%. To make it a truly apples-to-apples comparison, we apply the 1.5% expense ratio to the Roth IRA while letting the life insurance company illustration account for the internal expenses of the IUL. Next, we distribute tax-free dollars from both programs over another fixed time period (say 25 years) starting in year 11. By comparing the maximum cash flow that can be distributed over that time period, we begin to get a sense for the average fees of either program.

Year	Age	Roth Contribution	Roth Cash Flow	Roth Balance	Indexed Universal Life Contribution	IUL Cash Flow	IUL Balance	DB
1	51	10,000	0	10,589	10,000	0	9,201	189,778
2	52	10,000	0	21,801	10,000	0	19,005	199,582
3	53	10,000	0	33,673	10,000	0	29,411	209,988
4	54	10,000	0	46,244	10,000	0	40,526	221,103
5	55	10,000	0	59,556	10,000	0	52,401	232,978
6	56	10,000	0	73,651	10,000	0	65,045	245,622
7	57	10,000	0	88,576	10,000	0	78,534	259,111
8	58	10,000	0	104,380	10,000	0	92,927	273,504
9	59	10,000	0	121,114	10,000	0	108,288	288,865
10	60	10,000	0	138,833	10,000	0	124,685	305,262

[11] The IUL balances in these comparisons are taken from a real IUL illustration from a real life insurance company which, for compliance and legal purposes, shall go unnamed

[12] This example assumes a $5,000 Roth contribution for a husband and wife for a total annual contribution of $10,000

Year	Age	Roth Contribution	Roth Cash Flow	Roth Balance	Indexed Universal Life Contribution	Indexed Universal Life Cash Flow	Indexed Universal Life Balance	Indexed Universal Life DB
11	61	0	9,997	136,422	0	9,997	123,105	295,103
12	62	0	9,997	133,868	0	9,997	121,376	284,640
13	63	0	9,997	131,165	0	9,997	119,534	273,863
14	64	0	9,997	128,302	0	9,997	117,534	262,763
15	65	0	9,997	125,271	0	9,997	115,356	251,330
16	66	0	9,997	122,061	0	9,997	113,008	239,715
17	67	0	9,997	118,662	0	9,997	110,502	228,052
18	68	0	9,997	115,064	0	9,997	107,814	216,340
19	69	0	9,997	111,253	0	9,997	104,935	204,575
20	70	0	9,997	107,218	0	9,997	101,782	192,758
21	71	0	9,997	102,945	0	9,997	98,331	180,885
22	72	0	9,997	98,421	0	9,997	94,557	168,957
23	73	0	9,997	93,630	0	9,997	90,449	156,971
24	74	0	9,997	88,558	0	9,997	85,996	144,924
25	75	0	9,997	83,187	0	9,997	81,187	132,817
26	76	0	9,997	77,499	0	9,997	76,038	120,485
27	77	0	9,997	71,477	0	9,997	70,517	107,784
28	78	0	9,997	65,100	0	9,997	64,618	94,701
29	79	0	9,997	58,348	0	9,997	58,337	81,226
30	80	0	9,997	51,198	0	9,997	51,679	67,347
31	81	0	9,997	43,627	0	9,997	44,655	54,499
32	82	0	9,997	35,610	0	9,997	37,157	47,361
33	83	0	9,997	27,122	0	9,997	29,003	39,559
34	84	0	9,997	18,134	0	9,997	20,135	31,028
35	85	0	9,997	8,616	0	9,997	10,487	21,702

As you can see, the IUL actually distributed money just as productively over the 25-year period as the Roth IRA. If the IUL, in this case, has cash flow that's just as productive as the Roth IRA, then, by inference, it also has equal fees. It isn't important that the IUL's accumulation fund lags behind that of the Roth IRA initially, because ultimately, it distributes just as much income.

A second way to determine if your IUL has low fees is to determine its net internal rate of return (IRR) versus its tax-free alternative.

Internal Rate of Return (IRR)

The percentage rate earned on each dollar invested for each period it is invested. It gives an investor the means to compare alternative investments based on their yield.[13]

The IRR will show you what your investment's average cumulative expenses are in any given year. For example, if a Roth IRA always grows at 7.5% and has an expense ratio that's always 1.5%, then its IRR in any given year will always be 6%. Pretty straightforward, right?

Now let's look at a properly structured IUL. The IUL has an IRR that instead builds slowly over time. Why? Because the cost of life insurance as a percentage of the overall cash value is always the greatest in the early years. What you'll find, however, is that the IRR of a *properly structured* IUL, given enough time, will eventually catch up with and ultimately surpass that of your Roth IRA.

In the chart below, the IUL grows at an average gross rate of return of 7.5%. Notice how the IUL's IRR slowly builds and ultimately eclipses the Roth IRA's IRR (6%) in the 27th year.

---

[13] *Investopedia.com*

Year	Age	IRR
1	50	-58.55
2	51	-21.35
3	52	-9.68
4	53	-4.31
5	54	-1.39
6	55	0.38
7	56	1.55
8	57	2.41
9	58	3.04
10	59	3.52
11	60	4.11
12	61	4.53
13	62	4.85
14	63	5.10
15	64	5.29
16	65	5.44
17	66	5.54
18	67	5.62
19	68	5.70
20	69	5.76
21	70	5.81
22	71	5.85
23	72	5.89
24	73	5.92
25	74	5.95
26	75	5.98
27	76	6.01
28	77	6.03
29	78	6.06
30	79	6.08

Here's the big take away: since the IUL is a long-term proposition—again, we're talking about a marriage here—we shouldn't allow ourselves to become concerned with how it measures up to its tax-free alternatives in the short-term. Remember that IULs, like good marriages, work best if kept your entire life, 'till death do you part. The longer you keep your IUL, *the better it gets*. If you abandon your IUL in the short-term because you're afraid of what you think are high fees, you won't be around when things start to get really good. Like many good things in life, the IUL needs a chance to marinate. By showing patience and a bit of perspective, you unleash the IUL's productive force to do exactly what it was designed to do: build tax-free wealth safely and productively.

When comparing the fees between tax-free alternatives such as IULs and Roth IRAs, it all boils down to this: *whatever road you take in life, someone is going to be making 1.5%*. The real question is this: *What are you getting in exchange for that 1.5%?* In the case of the Roth IRA, you're primarily paying for the cost of money management. By the way, you pay those fees rain or shine, even in a down market. For example, if your money grows 30% in the stock market, what's the real net rate of return? That's right, 28.5%. And, if you lose 30% in the market, what's your total annual loss? Given an expense ratio of 1.5%, your total losses are 31.5%.

In the case of the IUL, you *are* paying 1.5% of your account value per year, on average, over the life of the program, but you're getting something very useful and impactful in exchange for it: a death benefit that doubles as long-term care (more on that in Chapter 5). You also get the prospect of safe *and* productive growth at a period in your life when you can't afford to endure a big financial squeeze: in retirement.

For the LIRP to be a productive part of your tax-free retirement approach, it must have fees as low as the tax-free alternatives you might have utilized had the LIRP not been in the picture. It's perfectly ok if your expenses are greater than 1.5% in the early years because those fees, when viewed as a percentage of your overall bucket, will fall dramatically over time. Also remember that you're getting something useful in exchange for those fees: safe and productive growth as well as a valuable death benefit that is usually not accounted for in "apples-to-apples" comparisons of the options. It is critical that your LIRP distribute money just as proficiently as the alternative tax-free approach. Properly structured, low-expense IULs from well-regarded companies satisfy these important criteria and are worthy of a long-term commitment.

Chapter 3: Questions to Consider

1. What is the relationship between fees and rate of return inside the LIRP?

2. How do you define "low fees" when it comes to the LIRP?

3. How do the fees inside a properly structured IUL compare to those of traditional retirement plans?

4. How does the internal rate of return inside a properly structured IUL change over time?

CHAPTER FOUR
TAX-FREE AND COST-FREE DISTRIBUTIONS

Now you have a sense of how important it is to choose a LIRP that delivers safe and productive growth in a low-fee environment. Without these two qualities, your LIRP relationship can be doomed from the start. Remember: this is like a marriage. Your decisions today will have lasting implications as you age and approach retirement. It's best to find out everything you can about your LIRP *now*, before you take the plunge and say, "I do."

As important as the above-mentioned qualities are, they can be quickly neutralized without a third critical attribute: tax-free *and* cost-free distributions. Now, I will happily remind you that every LIRP on the market qualifies as tax-free. But while every LIRP provides for tax-free distributions, these distributions often come at a cost, and these costs can ultimately land your LIRP marriage on the rocks. Before taking the LIRP leap, you must insist on having distributions that are both tax-free *and* cost-free.

The Tax-Free LIRP

Before we explore the benefits of cost-free distributions, let's revisit why LIRPs are tax-free in the first place. In *The Power of Zero* I explained

33

how distributions from LIRPs are only tax-free if taken out in the correct way. If you take a traditional distribution from a LIRP, like you might from a 401(k) or IRA, the money is construed as ordinary income and is taxable.[14] If you take the money out by way of a loan, however, the distribution is tax-free because the IRS doesn't consider loans to be taxable income.

When you take a loan from your LIRP, you're effectively taking a loan from the life insurance company itself. Here's how it works: you call up the company and say, "I'd like to take a loan for $10,000." They take $10,000 out of your growth account and put it into a loan collateral account where it earns a rate of interest. For this example we'll say 3%. In the very same transaction, the life insurance company sends you a loan from their own coffers. Now this is a loan, so you should expect it to come with an interest rate. Let's say that's also 3%. When you die, all the money in the loan collateral account is used to pay back the outstanding loan that you have with the company. If the interest charged on the loan is the same as the interest being credited in the loan collateral account, the net cost to you over the course of your lifetime is zero. In short, you asked for $10,000, you received $10,000 in the mail, your growth account went down by $10,000, and you never paid any tax. That's how distributions from your LIRP, when executed properly, qualify as tax-free.

Sounds Great … What Could Go wrong?

Now that you know how distributions from your LIRP can be tax-free, let's talk about some of the dangers that may crop up along the way. In a perfect world, the rate of interest the insurance company credits to the LIRP's loan collateral account is exactly the same as what they charge in the loan account. In other words, if they always credit you 3%, and they always charge you 3%, then the net cost to you will always be zero. Thus tax-free *and* cost free. However, some companies

---

[14] Any amount above and beyond a life insurance policy's basis is taxable when taking a traditional distribution

will guarantee to always credit you 3%, but reserve the right to charge you 4%, 5% or 6% at their sole discretion. Wait, what? I know, sounds a bit like having *their* fox in *your* chicken coop, right?

This actually happens more often than you'd think, and if you're not on top of your game, you may not even catch it when evaluating your LIRP alternatives. Here's how that situation might play out: let's say you enter into a LIRP relationship without reading the fine print. The life insurance company credits your loan collateral account 3% but decides to charge your loan account 5%. In this instance, the net cost for you to borrow is 2%. While 2% doesn't seem like such a big deal, especially when compared to the 35% taxes you might have otherwise paid in your taxable investment, it can actually be a major drag on the growth of your LIRP over time. Here's why: if you fail to pay that 2% interest back at the end of the year, the company will simply subtract it from your cash value. Then, if you take an additional loan in year 2, they'll charge you another 2%. Only, you haven't paid back the loan from year 1, so they'll charge you for that loan again! As you take additional loans from your policy, the interest owed continues to grow and compound. As it does, it creates a bigger and bigger drag on your cash value. If the cumulative expense of these loans overwhelms the growth of your LIRP, it can end up bankrupting your policy. In that case you would lose your death benefit *and* get a hefty tax bill from the IRS.

Tax Implications of Bankrupting Your LIRP

If you don't have at least $1 in your LIRP's cash value when you die, your policy loses its tax-free protection. As a result, all the taxes that you avoided along the way would come due in one year.

The following chart shows the massive costs that seemingly small loan provisions can exert on your cash value over the course of a 30-year retirement. Here I've compared a 2% and a 1% spread loan to a 0% spread loan:

Net Cost to Borrow Analysis			
Age 65 Cash Value $1,000,000			
Annual Loan: $75,000			
Rate of Growth: 7.5%			
Age	Year	2% Spread Loan	1% Spread Loan	0% Spread Loan
---	---	---	---	---
65	1	$75,000	$75,000	$75,000
66	2	$75,000	$75,000	$75,000
67	3	$75,000	$75,000	$75,000
68	4	$75,000	$75,000	$75,000
69	5	$75,000	$75,000	$75,000
70	6	$75,000	$75,000	$75,000
71	7	$75,000	$75,000	$75,000
72	8	$75,000	$75,000	$75,000
73	9	$75,000	$75,000	$75,000
74	10	$75,000	$75,000	$75,000
75	11	$75,000	$75,000	$75,000
76	12	$75,000	$75,000	$75,000
77	13	$75,000	$75,000	$75,000
78	14	$75,000	$75,000	$75,000
79	15	$75,000	$75,000	$75,000
80	16	$75,000	$75,000	$75,000
81	17	$75,000	$75,000	$75,000
82	18	$75,000	$75,000	$75,000
83	19	$75,000	$75,000	$75,000
84	20		$75,000	$75,000
85	21		$75,000	$75,000
86	22		$75,000	$75,000
87	23		$75,000	$75,000
88	24			$75,000

Age	Year	2% Spread Loan	1% Spread Loan	0% Spread Loan
89	25			$75,000
90	26			$75,000
91	27			$75,000
92	28			$75,000
93	29			$75,000
94	30			$75,000
Total Income		$1,425,000	$1,725,000	$2,250,000
Total Cost		$825,000	$525,000	$0

To the casual observer, 2% or 1% net loan provisions seem tiny, even insignificant. But the damage they can inflict over a 30-year period of time can be catastrophic. Consider the real cost of the 2% net loan provision shown above. Because of the compounding nature of loan interest, it bankrupts your policy 11 years early. That's a whopping $825,000 of loan income you lost because of a lousy 2% loan provision! The 1% loan provision doesn't fare much better. It only lasts four years longer and costs you an astounding $525,000 of lost loan income.

To add insult to injury, lousy loan provisions may, in the end, saddle you with a big tax bill. Here's why: if you weren't accounting for the additional drag on your growth account due to those extra loan charges, you may run out of money faster than you had anticipated. And again, if you run out of money before you die, you'll end up receiving that fat tax bill from the IRS. Remember, there has to be at least $1 in your cash value when you die or all of the taxes you avoided over the life of the policy come due, all in the same year. Here's the bottom line: if your LIRP has a lousy loan provision, it offsets many of the tax benefits that justified its use in the first place. When it comes to loan provisions, the devil is in the details. Make sure you've read the fine print!

So, Why *Do* Companies Have Lousy Loan Provisions?

In Chapter 1, we reviewed the three different accumulation strategies you can choose in order to grow your money inside your LIRP's
growth account. Since then, we've discussed the stock market-based
LIRP and the indexed-based LIRP (Indexed Universal Life). The third
accumulation strategy involves growing your money within the general investment portfolio of the insurance company. Companies that
sponsor these types of LIRPs aren't wild about giving you unfettered
access to cost-free policy loans. When you take a policy loan, the
money really comes out of their general investment portfolio which
means they no longer get to earn interest on it. With that in mind,
you really can't blame them for making the process difficult for you.
After all, insurance companies are businesses, so why would they give
you tax-free *and* cost-free access if it comes off of their bottom line?
To discourage these types of distributions, they will often charge a
rate of interest that's higher than what they credit your loan collateral
account. In fact, it isn't that unusual for the difference between those
two rates to be as high as 4%! Imagine the impact on your cash value
of a recurring and compounding net interest charge of 4%. It could
bankrupt your policy in short order!

Finding the Right Loan Provision

The best way to protect yourself against lousy loan provisions is to
make sure that the company that sponsors your LIRP gives themselves
as little wiggle room as possible. In a perfect world, you want the
amount they credit your loan collateral account and the amount they
charge for loans to always add up to 0%. If they can slap a guarantee
on that provision, all the better. Here's why: if a company guarantees
they will always credit your loan collateral account at 3% and they
guarantee they will always charge your loan account 3%, then the net
cost to you will *always* be 0%. Thus tax-free *and* cost-free, guaranteed
right in the contract. Remember, it's always tax-free per the IRS. But
the cost-free part is up to the insurance company. That's why it's so

important to educate yourself and ask informed questions. Be sure to do your LIRP research with your eyes wide open *before* tying the knot. There's nothing worse than discovering you have a locked-in 2% loan provision when you're 10 years into your LIRP marriage.

Can you see how safe and productive growth in a low-fee environment simply isn't enough when it comes to finding a suitable LIRP? A rock-solid, cost-free loan provision is foundational to your 0% retirement plan and it should be near the top of your LIRP laundry list. And the best news of all? All three of these indispensable attributes can be found in the right Indexed Universal Life policy.

Variable Loans

Now that you know how important it is to ensure that you're working with guaranteed, cost-free loan provisions, let's look at yet another option you will likely run into when looking for the right LIRP. Companies that offer Indexed Universal Life often have a second type of loan option that can be an attractive complement to the traditional cost-free loan provision. This is known as a variable loan. Now, right about now you might be thinking, why muddy the waters if you've already achieved perfection? How can you possibly improve upon tax-free *and* cost-free? Let's dig into exactly how these loans work, and once we have all the details laid out, *you* can be the judge.

Here's an example of how a variable loan might work for you: let's say you want to take a $10,000 loan from your IUL. Instead of crediting your loan collateral account at 3% (like with the traditional no-cost loan), the company credits whatever your index happened to earn that year. For example, if you were to have a successful year in which you maxed out your 13% cap, they would actually credit your loan collateral account at 13%!

On the flip side, the insurance company has to charge you something for the loan (as with the traditional no-cost loan), or the IRS will cry foul. The rate they typically charge can vary, but most companies currently charge between 5% and 6%.

So, if the company credited your loan collateral account at a rate of 13% in a given year, and they charged your loan account a rate of 6%, you would actually earn 7% just for taking a loan from your own policy! This is what we call a *positive loan arbitrage*. If the amount credited is consistently greater than the amount charged, then the company is effectively paying you to take a policy loan.

Now, there isn't an IUL out there that's going to average 13% per year, so it isn't realistic to expect a positive 7% loan arbitrage over the life of your policy. But if your IUL is consistently averaging 7.5%, and the loan charge holds steady at 6%, then you'd experience an average positive loan arbitrage of 1.5% over time. Again, we're talking small percentages that may not seem like a big deal at first glance, but when amortized over a lifetime, they can bring forth enormous dividends. The power of a 1.5% positive loan arbitrage can increase your tax-free distributions anywhere from 40% to 100%, depending on the variables involved.

If you want tax-free *and* cost-free distributions in retirement, it's imperative that you investigate your LIRP's loan provision *before* entering into a long-term commitment. The financial costs of overlooking this critical attribute can add up quickly. A few well-regarded IUL companies do offer the zero-cost option. By excluding all non-zero loan alternatives, you can quickly narrow the field of viable IUL candidates. Before settling on a specific IUL, however, go one step further and ensure that the company offers a variable loan provision as well. This alternative can help supercharge your growth account and dramatically increase cumulative loan distributions over the course of your retirement. Remember, the only LIRP that allows for both no-cost *and* variable loans is Indexed Universal Life.

Chapter 4: Questions to Consider

1   How can distributions from LIRPs be taken tax-free?

2   What is the difference between tax-free and cost-free?

3   What is the impact of a positive spread loan on a LIRP's cash value?

4   What happens if you bankrupt your LIRP before you die?

5   Why are zero-cost loans important in LIRP planning?

6   How do variable loans work?

7   Why can variable loans be a compelling feature in your LIRP?

CHAPTER FIVE

A LONG-TERM CARE RIDER

I f this is a book about identifying all of the indispensable qualities of the ideal LIRP, then why dedicate an entire chapter to long-term care? Simple: because a long-term care event may very well be the single most devastating event that could befall you in retirement (financially speaking, of course). When you find yourself in need of long-term care, the government requires that you spend down almost all of your assets before they'll step in and foot the bill. The lifestyle that you and your spouse had been planning and saving for no longer matters in the eyes of Uncles Sam. If you end up needing care, what may have been shaping up to be a rosy retirement could turn into a basic, bare-bones, subsistence lifestyle for your spouse.

Before delving into how the LIRP figures into the long-term care equation, we have to appreciate how truly devastating a long-term care event can be. To facilitate this, let's listen in on a conversation I have all too often with my clients:

Me: Mr. Jones, I'm going to have to tell you something that you might not want to hear.

Client: OK. Lay it on me.

Me: Don't take this the wrong way—we love you, but with regard to your finances, you're better off dying than needing long-term care.

Client: Go on.

Me: See, were you to die, all of your assets (your 401(k), IRA, mutual funds, etc.) would go to your wife, who is your beneficiary. And, while we would all miss you terribly, her life, from a financial perspective, would continue along relatively unchanged. However, if you didn't die but instead needed long-term care, all of a sudden, much of the money she was planning on using in retirement now gets earmarked for the long-term care facility.

At this point, if Mr. and Mrs. Jones haven't been fidgeting nervously, they are now.

Me: Here's how it works: before the Federal Government will step in to pick up the cost of your long-term care, your estate goes into what we call 'spend down.' Your wife becomes the 'community spouse' and is forced to spend down your estate until she's left with just one house, one car, a Minimum Monthly Maintenance Needs Allowance (MMMNA), which in most states averages around $2,500 a month, and $119,220 of cash. Then and only then will the Federal Government step in to pick up the bill.

By this time their eyes are like saucers and their mouths have fallen into their laps. Unfortunately, the conversation isn't quite over:

Me: Now, the same holds true for you Mrs. Jones. Were you to need long-term care, all of your and Mr. Jones' cumulative assets would go into spend down, and he would become the community spouse. He too may have to find a way to get by with only one house, one car, an MMMNA of $2500 a month, etc.

At first glance, this may seem a bit harsh or even insensitive, but when I find myself having to give this talk to my clients, this is pretty much how it goes down. They're trusting me with their finances, so I owe it to them to not pull any punches. The consequences of a long-term care event can just be too devastating.

I broach these types of conversations for two very important reasons:

1. **The Likelihood of a Long-Term Care Event:** The most recent statistics show that there's a 70% chance that at least one spouse will suffer a health event that requires long-term care.[15]

2. **The Costs of a Long-Term Care Event:** The expense of a long-term care event can, in a very short period of time, devour a lifetime of savings leaving the community spouse and their heirs financially devastated.[16]

These facts are well-documented. In fact, you likely have someone in your immediate or extended family who is currently dealing with the fall-out from a long-term care event. The question is, how do you go about mitigating such an insidious risk?

Historically, there have been only three ways to safeguard against this type of event:

1. **Self-Insure:** The idea here is that you accumulate such an enormous nest egg that you can afford to pay for the cost of long-term care for both you and your spouse out of pocket. While this may *seem* achievable, it's definitely not the best option for most people. Keep in mind that the average cost of long-term care is between $7,000 and $9,000 per month, per person.[17] At that rate, you could burn through a lifetime worth of savings in just a few short years!

2. **Rely on Family Members:** While this is an option to which some couples resort, experience shows that many children grow resentful when saddled with the prospect of taking care of an aging parent. Furthermore, the children lack the time, experience and know-how to provide the appropriate level of care.

[15] http://money.usnews.com/money/blogs/the-best-life/2011/04/11/5-reasons-you-need-a-long-term-care-plan

[16] http://www.wsj.com/articles/SB10001424052702303425504577352031401783756

[17] http://news.morningstar.com/articlenet/article.aspx?id=564139

3. **Buy a Long-Term Care Policy:** The other common alternative is to purchase a traditional long-term care policy in order to help offset the cost of long-term care. This usually kicks in when, as determined by a doctor, the insured can no longer perform 2 of the 6 activities of daily living, namely: eating, bathing, dressing, toileting, transferring (walking), and continence.

Based on these three options, it seems pretty clear that buying a long-term care policy is the easiest and most palatable way to mitigate this enormous financial risk. If that's the case, then why doesn't everyone have long-term care insurance? There are 4 main reasons:

1. **High Expense:** Long-term care insurance for a husband and wife can be pricey. Typical premiums for two 50 year olds can cost between $6,000 and $8,000 per year.

2. **Non-Guaranteed Premiums:** Not only is long-term care insurance expensive, but the premiums themselves aren't guaranteed. This is primarily because the cost of long-term care is hard to predict. Most companies offering these policies simply don't have enough claims experience to determine appropriate premiums. In order to cover their own bottom line (at the expense of yours), they reserve the right to make across-the-board rate increases on their policy holders.

3. **Hard to Qualify:** Qualification for a long-term care policy is based on morbidity (likelihood that you'll need long-term care), rather than mortality (longevity). You might very well live to be 120, but if you have a bad back, a bad knee, or other physical malady, you may be deemed "high risk" and not even qualify for a policy.

4. **Use-it-or-Lose-it Proposition:** Most people dread paying for something they hope they never have to use. With traditional long-term care insurance, if you die peacefully in your sleep 25 years from now never having needed the coverage, they don't send you your money back. The company keeps it and uses it to pay for someone else's benefit!

Remember, most couples do have plenty to gain by having long-term care insurance. It effectively wraps a huge layer of protection around your entire estate. These four roadblocks, however, tend to add up to one big, ugly case of heartburn for most prospective buyers. And that heartburn, in most cases, prevents them from ever pulling the trigger.

An Alternate Approach

Fortunately, there is an alternate way to protect your hard-earned retirement dollars from the drain of a long-term care event without all the heartburn that comes with traditional long-term care insurance. More importantly, this alternative allows for the possibility of getting long-term care coverage without the burden of onerous yearly premiums. As I often tell my clients, "Most people aren't opposed to having long-term care insurance. They're just opposed to paying for it!"

Think about it. If you could get all the benefits of long-term care coverage without actually having to pay for it, would it be a stressful decision? Of course not. If anything, you'd be asking if there was a "catch."

As it turns out, there's no catch at all. It simply involves maximizing the benefits of the right type of LIRP. To pull this off, you'll have to add one more quality to your laundry list of LIRP attributes: a long-term care rider. Happily, many well-regarded IUL carriers offer these types of riders.

Two Types of Long-Term Care Riders

Now I have to warn you: there are two main types of long-term care riders, only one of which fits the profile of what we're looking for. They are as follows:

1. **The Kind You Pay For**: The first type of long-term care rider actually costs you money. In other words, when you add this rider to your LIRP, your expenses actually get bigger. Here's how it works:

Let's say you have a $400,000 death benefit. You wake up one day and can no longer perform 2 of the 6 activities of daily living. If you can find a doctor who can write a letter to that effect, you'll start receiving 2% of your death benefit, or $8,000 per month, each and every month for 4 years. Sounds great, right? Well, there's one tiny problem with this type of approach. If you pay all those expenses all those years and die peacefully in your sleep never having needed long-term care, then you will have needlessly spent a lot of money along the way. You still haven't eliminated the #1 source of heartburn when it comes to long-term care insurance: paying for something you hope you'll never have to use! You're essentially back to square one.

2. **The Kind You Don't Pay For:** The second type of long-term care rider doesn't cost you a dime. There is, however, a significant difference. Companies still offer to pay you 2% of your death benefit over 4 years but they require that the amount be discounted. Let's use the example from above: You have a $400,000 death benefit and want to spend this money while you're alive for the purpose of paying for long-term care. The company will still calculate 2% of your death benefit, but before mailing you that check, the amount gets discounted. The discount typically works as follows: convert your age to a percentage, and then apply it to the $8,000 amount. For example, let's say that you're 75 years old when you need long-term care. That means that you'll get roughly 75% of that $8,000, or $6,000, each and every month for 4 years. I much prefer this approach to the first option. With this option, you get a smaller long-term care benefit, but if you die peacefully in your sleep never having needed it, you didn't lose any money along the way. You didn't needlessly subject your cash value to the drag of that additional long-term care expense. As a result, you get to spend more money in retirement.

Why Companies Discount

When a life insurance company underwrites you for a policy, they are essentially trying to predict how long you're going to live. This helps them gauge the actual costs of insuring you over a lifetime. If they think you'll live a long life, they'll charge you less, because they know they'll be collecting those expenses over a longer period of time. If they think you'll live a short life, they'll charge you more because they have less time in which to collect those expenses.

Let's say that after a thorough underwriting process, a company predicts that you'll live to age 90. Let's also say that at age 75, you end up needing long-term care. If they were to give you your *entire* death benefit starting at age 75, then they would lose out on the expenses they might otherwise have earned had they waited until age 90 to pay out your death benefit. By discounting the portion of the death benefit they send you each month for long-term care purposes, they're able to cover the cost of those lost expenses.

Paying for Life Insurance with Already Budgeted Dollars

At this point, you may be thinking, *I thought you said the long-term care coverage was free! If the life insurance company is merely giving me my death benefit in advance of my death for the purpose of paying for long-term care, I'm still paying for it. I'm just getting it a little early.*

To see where I'm going with this, consider the following: if you're preparing for a tax-free retirement, as discussed in *The Power of Zero*, there's a good chance your plan calls for shifting money from your tax-deferred bucket to your tax-free bucket. If that's the case, there's also a good chance that you'll be peeling off a portion of that shift and using it to fund your IUL. If the money being used to fund your IUL is coming from an IRA, then you are already accustomed to paying an annual fee of around 1.5%. You may recall from Chapter 3 that the average annual expense over the life of a properly structured IUL is also 1.5% per year. So, instead of spending 1.5% on the mutual fund fees from your IRA, you're now using it to pay for the average annual costs of an IUL. You're using money that's already been earmarked for one kind of expense to pay for a different kind of expense altogether: the cost of life insurance that doubles as long-term care.

Here's the moral of the story: whichever road you take in life, somebody's going to be making 1.5%. You just have to evaluate what you're getting in exchange for that 1.5%. In the IUL, you get safe and productive growth, tax-free and cost-free distributions, and a death benefit that covers your neck in the event you should need long-term care. Talk about making your 1.5% work hard!

Statistically speaking, there's a high chance that you or your spouse will need long-term care at some point during your retirement. This likelihood is much greater than a premature death or even disability, and its effects can be more devastating. Most people want to mitigate the effects of a long-term care event; they just don't like the heartburn associated with the traditional means of doing so. Long-term care insurance is expensive, hard to qualify for, and presents a use-it-or-lose-it proposition. Finding an IUL with a cost-free long-term care rider can be an effective, angst-free way to help mitigate that insidious risk. As you go about your IUL courtship process, insist that this feature occupy a prominent spot on your rapidly growing laundry list of qualities vital to a happy and enduring LIRP partnership.

Chapter 5: Questions to Consider

1. Why is a long-term care event perhaps the most devastating event that could befall you in retirement?

2. What are the 3 ways people traditionally pay for long-term care expenses?

3. What are the 4 pitfalls of traditional long-term care insurance?

4. How can a LIRP be used to pay for long-term care expenses?

CHAPTER SIX

CREATING YOUR IUL
LAUNDRY LIST

Thus far, we've made the case that there is only one LIRP that is best suited to help propel you into the 0% tax bracket in retirement, and that's Indexed Universal Life. The other types of LIRPs have virtues in their own rights, but when it comes to zero-tax retirement planning, the IUL simply does the best job, end of story. If that's the case then, why read any further? The reality is that, just as not all LIRPs are created equal, neither are all IULs created equal. To forge the right LIRP partnership, one with which you'll be happy for your entire retirement, we have to drill down even further. Just because an IUL is safe and productive, low-cost, has tax-free and cost-free distributions, and has a free long-term care rider, it doesn't mean you should throw caution to the wind. Even after all these considerations, there is still a substantially wide abyss that separates the good IULs from the bad ones.

This chapter will help you bridge that abyss, while refining your understanding of what constitutes an ideal LIRP. Remember, nobody wants to get married only to find out years into the relationship that their spouse is not as advertised. The time for uncovering skeletons and other unseemly surprises is now, before you tie the knot, not years into the marriage. Trying to divorce your LIRP can be emotionally exhausting, time intensive, and expensive. Make sure you compile an "IUL laundry list"—just like you did with the LIRP in general—well before you get to the altar. This is the final step before you take the big leap. So, sharpen your pencil, grab that list, and let's get started!

#1: Guaranteed 0% Loans

As we learned in Chapter 4, one of the single most important components in your IUL is the loan provision. As you may have guessed, this is the provision that governs the cost of taking tax-free distributions from your IUL. Remember, all loans from all life insurance policies are tax-free. That's just the nature of loans. But they're not all cost-free. When you take a loan from your IUL, the company takes money out of your growth account, deposits it into a loan collateral account and credits you a rate of interest. At the same time, they cut you a check from their own coffers and charge you a stated rate of interest. Ideally, you want the amount that they charge you and the amount that they credit you to be exactly the same amount. That's how we get tax-free *and* cost-free. In a perfect world, you also want the amount that they charge you and the amount that they credit you to be guaranteed. Remember, if the company has the ability to increase your loan interest rate at their leisure, then *their* fox is in *your* chicken coop!

Having said all of this, only a few companies guarantee that these two numbers will always be equal. Some companies, however, guarantee that the difference between these two numbers will never be worse than .25%. While a guaranteed .25% net loan interest rate is not perfect, it's far superior to a loan provision which gives the life insurance company the latitude to raise your loan rate by an astounding 4%! It wouldn't take long for a 4% loan provision to sink your LIRP's ship!

A Tale of Two Loan Provisions

A good loan provision charges no net interest to the client, but is also worded in a clear and unambiguous way. A bad loan provision, on the other hand, not only has a net cost, but can be shrouded in legalese, nebulous terms, and convenient escape clauses.

Consider the following zero-cost loan provision:

"After the 5th policy year, We guarantee that We will offer zero-cost loans. The annual interest rate charged on zero-cost loans is guaranteed to be 3.5% (which is the same rate We guarantee to credit on zero-cost loans)."

Notice how the amount being credited is exactly the same as the amount being charged starting on the first day of the 6th year. What's more, the word "guarantee" is used on *three* separate occasions! This is a classic example of an iron-clad, guaranteed 0% loan provision.

Contrast that with the following example of a non-zero-cost loan:

"The annual interest rate on a Policy loan will be 8% for the first 10 Policy Years, 7% for Policy Years 11 through 20 and 6.50% for Policy Years 21 and later. We guarantee we will credit the Loan Account at 6%. The maximum guaranteed net cost of loans is 2% (annually) and may be less."

Wait, what? Be honest, how many times did you go back and re-read that to see if you could figure out exactly what was going on? Let's break it down and see if we can decipher the implications for the policy holder. At first glance, it appears that the loan charge over the first 20 years will drop from 8% to 7%, and then ultimately to 6.5%. It also appears that the company guarantees that they'll credit the loan collateral account (Loan Account) at 6%. So, on the surface, the worst case scenario appears to be a net .50% loan cost after the 20th year (a 6.5% loan charge minus a 6% loan credit). However, note the very last sentence. "The maximum guaranteed net cost of loans is 2% (annually) and may be less." In other words, notwithstanding everything they told you in the first two sentences, the worst case loan provision could *still* be as high as 2%! They *intend* to reduce the loan charge from 8% to 6.5% over the first 20 years, but they're not willing to guarantee it. It *may* result in a .50% loan provision, but then again, it may not. The policy holder has no assurances. Are you beginning to see how the devil is in the details when it comes to these loan provisions?

In short, before making a long-term commitment to your IUL, make it a point to closely examine the policy's loan provision. If you see that the amount credited and the amount charged are the same, then there's a reasonable likelihood that you have a good loan provision. However, if the loan credit and charge are both guaranteed to be the same, then you can have confidence that your IUL will be a reliable tax-free *and* cost free stream of income in retirement.

#2: Caps on Variable Loan Interest Charges

In Chapter 4, we discussed a second loan option for your IUL: variable loans. Variable loans are worth serious consideration because they can potentially increase cumulative loan distributions from your IUL anywhere from 40% to 100%. As you may recall, there are two primary differences between this type of loan and the guaranteed 0% wash loans. First, instead of crediting your loan collateral account with a fixed rate (say 3%), they credit it with whatever rate your accumulation account happened to get that year (say 13%). Second, instead of charging you a fixed rate in your loan account, they charge you a rate that can rise and fall with the London Inter-Bank Offered Rate (LIBOR). Here's where things can get a little dicey if you don't do your research ahead of time. Remember, if you elect a variable loan, and your index goes down in a given year, then your loan collateral account gets credited 0%. If, on the other side of the ledger, you're being charged 10% for your loan (based on the LIBOR), then you would end up having to pay a net 10% interest charge from your cash value. You'd be better off taking a loan from your bank or your home equity line of credit!

The competitive IUL companies, however, put a cap on the rate they can charge annually for your variable loans, regardless of how high the LIBOR goes. Acceptable caps on variable loan charges can range anywhere from 5% to 6%. So, for example, if you consistently get a 7.5% return in your index, and your company consistently charges you a maximum guaranteed 6% for your variable loan, then you'll experience a positive loan arbitrage of 1.5%. In other words, they'd actually be paying you 1.5% to take that loan. If the variable loan is a provision you're looking for in an IUL, make sure the life insurance company has a low cap on their loan rate so as to increase the likelihood of a positive loan arbitrage.

#3: Interest in Arrears

There's one other seemingly inconsequential but important detail when it comes to your IUL's loan provision. The interest on these preferred loan provisions can be charged in two different ways. Let's define them:

1. **Interest in Arrears:** In this scenario the life insurance company charges your accumulation account for the cost of the loan 12 months after you've taken the loan.

2. **Interest in Advance:** Here the life insurance company charges your accumulation account for the cost of the loan on the very same day you ask for it.

When is the Interest Charged?

Fortunately, the wording that insurance companies use to distinguish between interest in arrears and interest in advance is much easier to understand than the main guts of the loan provision itself. It's customary to see these provisions described in the following way:

Interest in Arrears:

"Interest is due at the end of each policy year."

Interest in Advance:

"We charge interest for a Policy Loan on the day we process the Policy Loan."

It seems pretty straightforward, right? Either you pay now, or you pay later. All things being equal, wouldn't the fiscally responsible choice be to pay up front and be done with it?

Not so. In theory, it's nice to not have to worry about impending costs, but in practice, you'd actually do well to put this one off. The difference between how these two interest charging methods function in the real world comes down to that now familiar—and important—concept of opportunity cost. Remember the impact of opportunity cost and how a loss is not just a loss? If you give someone a dollar that you didn't really need to give them, not only do you lose that dollar, but you lose what that dollar could have earned for you had you been able to keep it and invest it for the rest of your life.

Interest in advance, unfortunately, is rife with opportunity cost. If the insurance company subtracts the cost of the loan (say 3%) from your growth account at the beginning of the year, you lose the opportunity to earn interest on that 3% over the course of that year. Had your entire growth account grown 13% that year, then that 3% would have missed out on all that growth!

While this may seem inconsequential in the big scheme of things, the cumulative effect of an "interest in advance" loan provision can add anywhere from .2% to .6% to your net cost of borrowing. So, what may appear on the surface to be a "no-cost" loan can actually cost you as much as .6%! And, while a .6% loan provision is far superior to 4%, those snowballing expenses may cause you to run out of money much quicker than you anticipated. Remember, if you don't have at least $1 left in your growth account when you die, you'll get a massive 1099 from the IRS!

When it comes to loan provisions, the devil is in the details. Once you've identified a company that offers a loan provision that's at or near a guaranteed 0%, insist on having your interest charged in arrears. While there is a bit of extra leg work that goes into deciphering these loan provisions, having these qualities in place will go a long way towards ensuring a successful IUL marriage.

#4: A Stable Index Cap Rate

Have you ever jumped at a credit card rate that offered an impossibly low 9.9% introductory rate only to see that rate shoot through the roof once the honeymoon period was over? Chances are you proceeded a little more circumspectly the next time you got one of those offers in the mail. Well, the same type of caution should be exercised when evaluating the index caps of an Indexed Universal Life policy. Keep in mind that most well-regarded IUL companies offer index caps from 12% to 15%. Caps in this range allow you to truly participate in the upward movement of that stock market index, while at the same time enjoying the down-side protection of a 0% floor. Think of the implications, for example, of having only a 4% cap during a year in which the S&P 500 grew 20%. You'd be kicking yourself! One of the most attractive features of the IUL would have been rendered moot!

So, it's imperative that you have a cap that's consistently in the 12% to 15% range. Occasionally you'll see companies that offer a vertigo-inducing, gravity-defying 17% rate. This is a classic example of where it pays to "look before you LIRP." Remember, companies like to give themselves lots of wiggle room when it comes to index cap rates, so there's a high degree of likelihood that stratospheric 17% cap will come crashing back down to earth sometime soon after the first year. I've seen instances where companies offered an 18% cap rate only to drop it to 11% or worse soon thereafter. Not much different than how credit card companies lure you in with deceptive introductory rates!

The name of the game when it comes to caps is stability. If the IUL you're looking at, for example, has a 14% cap, take a look at where that cap rate was the prior year, and the year before that. Do they throw out teaser rates just to get people through the doors, or do they start with more realistic cap rates and keep them level, stable and sustainable? I'd much prefer to have a 13% cap rate year after year than to start at a 20% cap only to fall to a 9% cap when the honeymoon was over.

The reason stable cap rates are important is that for every full point that your cap gets lowered (i.e. from 14% to 13%), your average rate of return over time gets eroded by .4%. So, if a company lures you in with a cap of 17%, and then drops it to 10%, they've reduced the average annual return of your IUL by 2.8% (7% multiplied by .4%).

Before jumping into an IUL with an impossibly high cap, insist on seeing the company's track record. If they have a history of wildly volatile cap rates, then it's best to move along and keep on shopping. If their cap rates, conversely, have hovered in that 12% to 15% range over an extended period of time, then you may have found the stability that justifies a long-term commitment.

#5: A Financially Stable Company

Have you ever heard someone say that all squares are rectangles, but not all rectangles are squares? Well, that's a fairly apt analogy when discussing the life insurance company that sponsors your IUL. Here's what I mean: all good IULs are sponsored by financially stable life insurance companies *but* not all financially stable life insurance companies have good IULs. In other words, you can have an IUL that possesses all of the attributes we've discussed to this point, but if it's sponsored by a financially unstable company, then it's all for naught. After all, if your

IUL company goes broke, who cares about guarantees they can no longer honor? On the flip side, you could have an extremely financially stable life insurance company that offers an IUL with high expenses, low index caps and prohibitive loan provisions.

To make all this work, we're going to have to align the stars. We're looking for all of the favorable attributes we've discussed to this point, all under the umbrella of a financially stable, rock-solid company.

So how do we judge whether a life insurance company is truly rock-solid? There are four main organizations that rate life insurance companies: Moody's, Standard & Poor's, A.M. Best, and Fitch. The problem is, they each have their own methods for rating insurance companies, and making heads or tails of their rankings can sometimes be confusing. For example, an A+ rating with A.M. Best is the second best rating. But, with Standard & Poor's or Fitch an A+ is the fifth best rating. For that reason, I prefer an independent ranking service known as Comdex. Comdex averages the rankings of the above mentioned companies and comes up with a composite score of anywhere from 1 to 100. This ranking works a little like those tests we used to take back in high school. Remember when they said you were in the 92nd percentile in math? That basically meant that you were in the top 8% of the students. In other words, your math proficiency was better than 92% of your peers. Well, the same holds true with the Comdex ranking system. If the Comdex score of a life insurance company is 90, then it's more financially stable than 90% of the life insurance companies in the industry. Given what I've seen with life insurance companies over the years, it's critical that you limit your search to IUL companies that have a Comdex rating of 85 or better.

#6: An Over-Loan Protection Rider

Historically, there has been one well-documented shortcoming with the IUL (and LIRPs in general): if you don't have at least $1 left in your growth account when you die, all the taxes that you avoided having to pay because of the protections that life insurance enjoys, come due in one year. Now, IULs *are* impervious to market loss, but that alone does not guarantee protection against this pitfall. There are other circumstances that can prematurely deplete your cash value and force you to deal with this nightmare scenario. They include:

1. **Increased Insurance Expenses:** If an insurance company suffers a major financial setback, they reserve the right to increase the cost of insurance among their policy holders to keep from going bankrupt. Back in the 1980s, some life insurance companies got caught up in the junk bond crisis and did just that to keep their financial statements flush. While this can be good for the insurance company's bank account, it's disastrous for the policy holder. When the policy's expenses are greater than the growth of your cash value, then your growth account essentially bleeds out until you're broke. This generally isn't a problem if we adhere to item #5 on our IUL laundry list, but it bears mentioning.

2. **Over-Zealous Policy Loans:** If an IUL policy holder takes so many loans that the amount of money remaining in the growth account is not enough to sustain the expenses coming out, then the policy holder risks running out of money. This isn't typically a problem if the IUL is only one of multiple streams of tax-free income, but again, it's worth mentioning.

3. **Lack of Growth:** If the growth of the IUL's expenses (as the policy holder ages) outstrips the growth of the IUL's cash value due to lackluster performance or prohibitively low caps, then the policy could, potentially, run out of cash prematurely. This can be prevented if we adhere to item #4 on our IUL laundry list.

Within the last ten years, some insurance companies have mitigated this Achilles heel by adding a powerful little provision to their policies known as the "over-loan protection rider." This rider simply says that if the insured has held the policy long enough (say 10 years) and the cash value in the policy falls low enough (due to excessive loans, excessive expenses, lack of growth, or all three), then the insurance company will give you the option of activating the over-loan protection feature of the policy. When this happens, the insurance company reduces the death benefit to the point where the remaining cash value within the policy "pays the policy up." At this point, you no longer have the ability to take money out of the policy, but you avoid ever having to receive that huge tax for effectively outliving your IUL. Because the policy is paid up, you're also guaranteed to get a death benefit, even if it is somewhat reduced. The net effect of this rider is to completely neutralize the single greatest danger to your IUL. Before making any final decisions on your IUL, make sure this vital safeguard is part of the contract.

#7: Daily or Weekly Sweeps

What's a sweep, you must surely be thinking, *and why should I care how often it happens?* When you contribute money to your IUL, it gets immediately deposited into an account where it earns a nominal rate of interest. From that account the life insurance company "sweeps" your contribution into the growth account where it immediately goes to work for you. Most well-regarded IUL companies execute this sweep either on a daily or a weekly basis. Whether it's daily or weekly doesn't matter all that much in the grand scheme of things. There are some life insurance companies, however, that only sweep this account on a quarterly, semi-annual or even an annual basis! During the period of time before your money gets "swept," your money simply languishes in a state of limbo, losing out on the growth it might otherwise have received had it been put immediately to work in your growth account. Remember opportunity cost? If every time you make a contribution to your IUL, it sits idle for anywhere from 3 months to a year before being invested, you end up paying a huge price in lost growth poten-tial. When you amortize these seemingly insignificant delays out over a lifetime, you begin to see a dangerous drag on the growth of your money. Be absolutely certain that your IUL has either a daily or weekly sweep before diving into a long-term commitment.

Although the IUL is the ideal LIRP to help you accomplish your zero-tax retirement plan, not just any IUL will do. The discrepancies between IULs can be as stark as the differences between cars, computers or even vacuum cleaners, and you owe it to yourself to do just as much research with your prospective IUL as you would any other product. In short, all IULs are *not* created equal! By adhering to the IUL laundry list in this chapter, you can protect yourself against the hidden pitfalls and nasty surprises that can exact a cost on your LIRP marriage at a period in your life when you can least afford to pay it: in retirement!

Chapter 6: Questions to Consider

1. In what ways are all IULs not created equal?

2. Why can it be dangerous to not have a guaranteed zero-cost loan?

3. What are the dangers of having variable loan charges without caps?

4. What is the difference between interest in arrears and interest in advance?

5. Why are high first-year loan caps not necessarily a good thing?

6. How do Comdex ratings work and why are they important when considering a LIRP?

7. Why is an over-loan protection rider important?

8. In what ways can an IUL's cash value be prematurely depleted?

9. What are "sweeps" and why is their frequency important?

CHAPTER SEVEN
THE TOP 10 IUL MYTHS

O ver the last 10 years IULs have emerged as a top LIRP choice for the laundry list of reasons we've already covered. As the IUL has grown in popularity, however, it has attracted the attention of many so-called "financial gurus," from columnists to former financial planners to pretty much anyone with an internet connection. Not surprisingly (it is the internet, after all) some of their opinions can get rather nasty. The problem, though, isn't so much nastiness as it is misinformation. Financial gurus have a penchant for dispensing one-size-fits-all financial planning advice that can fly in the face of the tax-free paradigm. Consider the following advice from a popular, mainstream financial guru:

> *"If your employer matches your contributions to your 401(k), 403(b), TSP, then invest up to the match. Next, fully fund a Roth IRA for you (and your spouse, if married). If that still doesn't total 15% of your income, come back to the 401(k), 403(b) or TSP."*[18]

Let's break this down. This guru recommends contributing to your 401(k) up to the match (so far so good), then your Roth IRAs (love

[18] *daveramsey.com*

it), and if you still have money left over, go back to the 401(k) again, contributing above and beyond the match (aaahhhhhhhhh!!!).

This guru clearly didn't read *The Power of Zero*. There is no mention whatsoever of the implications of having too much money in your tax-deferred bucket in a rising-tax rate environment or the resulting impact on Social Security taxation. It's little surprise that this same guru doesn't seem to understand or appreciate the role that a properly structured IUL can play in helping you get into the 0% tax bracket in retirement.

Financial gurus often find themselves on the outside of the tax-free paradigm looking in, trying to interpret what they're seeing through the lens of their "tax-deferred" world view. And while their intentions are often noble, their recommendations, if accepted at face value, can lead to a cascade of financial consequences, many of which may prevent you from ever reaching the 0% tax bracket.

To help you meet this sort of bad advice head-on, I've compiled a list of the 10 most common IUL myths, many of which stem from financial gurus' main-stream, tax-deferred views of personal finance. While it's easy to throw out pithy sound bites and verbal hand grenades when it comes to the IUL, the truth is often much harder to come by. With that in mind, let's dive into some of these myths and address them in a balanced, open and fair-minded way.

Myth #1: Be Wary of Overly Optimistic IUL Illustrations!

When an advisor gives you a recommendation for an IUL, they are legally required to show you an illustration. These illustrations show the performance of the IUL based on a number of different variables, among the most important of which is the rate of return. Some critics suggest that the rates of return shown on these illustrations are too high and unrealistic.

Let's look closer into the root of the claim, though. Are the rates of return that advisors project for IULs not based in reality? As we learned in Chapter 2, IULs have been around since about the year 2000, so we have a full 15 years to test the track record of its unique crediting method: participating in rising markets while protecting against downside loss. During that time period the market has been nothing short of a roller coaster ride. That notwithstanding, some well-regarded IUL companies have recorded actual, verifiable rates of return of well over 7.5% during that time period.

At this point, critics often cry foul. "Fifteen years simply isn't enough time to judge the viability of the IUL's crediting method," they say. For that reason, insurance companies provide historical back testing. These tests show how the IUL might have fared, given current variables, had it been around over the last 20, 25, 30 or 40 years. Leading insurance companies have consistently shown through backtested results that IULs would still have averaged well over 7.5% per year during each of these time periods.

Some critics, however, will not be placated, insisting that 40 years of historical back-testing does not a track record make. The last 40 years, they maintain, have been an unprecedented bull market not likely to be repeated in the future. Keep in mind, however, that the last 40 years also includes that hyper-volatile period of the last 15 years, a period in which we saw flat markets, bull markets, bear markets and arguably the worst financial crisis since the Great Depression. Yet, the *actual* returns of many well-regarded IULs during that 15-year time period were over 7.5%! In short, whether we're using historical back testing or actual, verifiable track records, many IULs do not, in fact, "over-promise and under-deliver" as some financial gurus claim.

Myth #2: Flexible Index Caps Should Have You Thinking Twice about IULs

Well-regarded IUL companies provide caps of anywhere from 12% to 15%, but do reserve the right to lower those caps at any point. While it's true that caps may be lowered, we have to understand the circumstances that might lead an insurance company to do so. Index caps are determined by the price of the underlying options that insurance companies use to help the client participate in the upside of the market. The cost of these options ebbs and flows based on the VIX index (or fear index) which measures the volatility or unpredictability in the stock market. When the stock market is volatile, it becomes less predictable, and the cost of these options goes up. To compensate for the rising cost of these options, insurance companies lower their caps.

Here is another case in which the relatively short history of IULs helps shed light on the question of cap variability. Between 2000 and 2015, we saw stock market rates of return zig-zagging all over the board. If ever there were a testing ground for how index caps might respond to rough market conditions, that was it. Even in the wake of the 2008-2009 financial crisis, some IUL companies only lowered their cap by 1%! In short, for insurance companies to lower their caps to the point where we might begin to worry, the stock market would have to be *even more* volatile and unpredictable than it has been over the last 15 years.

Additionally, as I tell my own clients, whatever road you take in your financial lives is fraught with peril. Your 401(k) could lose 50% in one year, your real estate values could collapse, and, in theory, your IUL company *could* lower its caps. You must recognize the risk inherent in every financial alternative (however small in the case of the IUL) and follow the course that gives you the greatest opportunity for safe *and* productive returns.

Myth #3: Avoid IULs Because of Non-Guaranteed Insurance Expenses

After having given your IUL illustration a look-over, you may come back to the table with misgivings about the "guaranteed" column of that illustration. This column reflects the "worst case scenario," the limit beyond which the insurance company cannot legally raise the cost of insurance. While these expenses are staggeringly high and make any illustration look rather dire, we find ourselves right back in the same territory we explored in Myth #2. Could the worst-case scenario happen? Certainly. Is it likely to? Probably not.

While every company does reserve the right to revert to a worst-case scenario, and is legally bound to disclose it up front, we have to weigh this likelihood versus the risk of not utilizing the IUL's benefits at all. Many well-regarded IUL companies haven't had to revert to these expenses in any of their products at any time in the last 100 years. So, while insurance companies do reserve the right to charge these expenses should people start dying at a much more accelerated rate (i.e., WWIII, pandemic, etc.), it is not a likely scenario. The likelihood of having a repeat market performance of 2008 is much greater by comparison (in turn, creating a greater need for the down-side protection of the IUL). Further, should insurance companies revert to guaranteed expenses, policy holders reserve the right to do a tax-free 1035 exchange of their surrender value into an annuity, effectively terminating the policy and eliminating those expenses.

Myth #4: Beware of the IUL's Non-Guaranteed Death Benefit

Critics claim that, while many IULs do have death benefit guarantees that stretch as long as 15 years, these guarantees expire at a time in the client's life when they need the death benefit the most: when they are older and more likely to die. There are a few issues here. First of all, many insurance companies offer IULs with death benefit guarantees all the way to age 120. Second, the vast majority of clients who utilize an IUL do so because they are planning on taking money out in retirement. Guess what? Even if your IUL did have a death benefit guarantee, you run the risk of voiding it the minute you take money out of the policy. So, if you are planning on drawing from your IUL to support your lifestyle in retirement, then the death benefit guarantee can often be a moot point.

Here's the bottom line: if you're interested in a death benefit guarantee *and* the ability to take tax-free policy loans in retirement, then the smart move would be to set up two policies--one that provides a death benefit guarantee and whose cash value will not be touched, and another that is designed to build wealth that can be distributed as tax-free supplementary income in retirement.

Myth #5: The IUL Has High Fees!

In *The Power of Zero* I addressed the question of whether or not LIRPs have high fees. What I said there does apply specifically to IULs. Here's an excerpt:

> *Do LIRPs really have high fees? If so, compared to what? To establish a baseline, I decided to look at the average fees for America's most popular retirement account: the 401(k). According to USA Today, the total expenses for a typical 401(k) plan are about 1.5% of the entire account balance per year. These fees go to pay record keepers, financial advisors, and mutual fund managers. In practical terms, this means that if your account's growth were 8% in a given year, your statement would show a net growth of only 6.5%.*
>
> *Now that we have a baseline, we can see how the average fees in an LIRP stack up by comparison. Generally speaking, the fees in an LIRP are higher in the early years and lower in the later years. Considered over the life of the program, however, these fees can average as little as 1.5%.*
>
> *The key to attaining this low level of expense lies in the proper structuring of the LIRP contract from the outset. To maximize cash accumulation and minimize expense, the contract must contain as little life insurance as possible while being funded at the highest level allowed under IRS guidelines. This "maximum-funding" scenario ensures that the level of expenses, as a percentage of the overall contributions, remains as low as possible.[19]*

Again, just because a "financial guru" says that an IUL has high fees doesn't make it so. When fees are averaged out over the policy holder's lifetime, the IUL is revealed to be a cost effective way to build tax-free wealth while providing death benefit and long-term care protection.

[19] McKnight, David; *The Power of Zero*, 2014, Acanthus Publishing, pages 43-44

Myth #6: Taking Loans from an IUL in a Flat Market Is Risky

Some so-called financial gurus warn that taking distributions from an IUL in a flat market can be dangerous. The thinking is that even if an IUL can never do worse than 0%, it still has to sustain the cost of insurance in those flat years. If you couple policy loans with the cost of insurance in a flat year, your policy could go into a tail-spin from which it may be difficult to recover.

Assuming for a second that this were a likely scenario, you'd have to make some rather non-guru-like decisions to fall victim to it. I've long advocated that distributions from the IUL should be one of multiple streams of tax-free income upon which clients rely in retirement. When coupled with Roth IRAs, Roth 401(k)s, Roth Conversions and tax-free distributions from IRAs (up to the standard deduction and personal exemptions), tax-free distributions from an IUL can be a welcome *supplement* to a tax-free retirement. Should an IUL not perform well in any given year, this might be the ideal time to avail yourself of your other tax-free streams of income. The peril arises when you put all your eggs into the IUL basket and fail to diversify your sources of tax-free income.

Myth #7: The IUL Shifts the Risk of Growing Cash Value to the Policyholder

This is an argument commonly put forth by advocates of LIRPs whose growth accounts are tied to the general investment portfolio of the insurance company. While these types of policy holders shift the onus of growing their money onto the insurance company, IUL policy holders assume the "risk" themselves. They do so by linking the growth of their accumulation account to any of 6 to 8 different stock market indexes. So the success of an IUL, the story goes, ultimately depends on the policy holder's ability to choose the "right" indexes.

Most financial advisors with whom I associate advocate a balance of at least two or three different indexes (for diversification purposes), each of which has back-tested rates of return that range from 7% to 9% over the last 40 years. For our purposes, let's assume these mixes of indexes continue to provide a 7.5% average annual rate of return into the future. Let's also assume these contracts are properly structured (by minimizing the death benefit and maximizing contributions up to IRS guidelines) and have average internal expenses over the life of the program of 1.5%. After subtracting expenses, that's an average net rate of return of 6%. Getting a consistent 6% net rate of return without taking any more risk than what you're accustomed to taking in your savings account is not an inherently risky proposition. Once again, we make financial decisions every day that involve risk. Having to choose the right complement of indexes in your IUL with the help of your financial advisor should not be considered one of them.

Myth #8: The IUL's Minimum Interest Rate Guarantees Are Smoke in Mirrors

Some critics suggest that the IUL's minimum interest rate guarantee isn't what it's cracked up to be. Before addressing their concerns, let's discuss how these guarantees work and when they come into play. Some IUL companies offer their policy holders a minimum guaranteed growth rate of between 2% and 3%. That doesn't mean, however, that they guarantee you'll receive a 2% to 3% credit in all down years. As is usual in the financial world, it's a bit more complex than that. Let's break it down.

One such guarantee might work in the following way: Every 5 years (usually between 5 and 8 years, depending on the company), the company looks back at the growth in your accumulation account and asks: Did your money grow at a minimum cumulative rate of at least 2% over those 5 years? If not, they will go back and retroactively credit (or in industry parlance "true up") your account at a 2% cumulative rate for each of those 5 years. In other words, the worst your policy will grow over any 5 year period is 2%.

Why do insurance companies make these guarantees? Firstly, it's a matter of marketing. It sure sounds nice to have a guaranteed return, even if it's a paltry 2%. But if you dig deeper into *how* they can guarantee 2%, it all points back to the productive nature of a good IUL. Given the performance of these policies over any historical 5-year period, what's the likelihood that the index would be down in so many of those years as to average only 2%? Not very likely. The market would have to experience very little movement (or go straight down) consistently over that 5-year period which the market rarely does. Even during the "lost decade" of the 2000s (where the market finished the decade pretty close to where it started) there were incredibly wide swings in the market which resulted in huge gains for IUL policies. In short, the IUL's critics are wasting a lot of hot air on a perceived deficiency that has a very low statistical likelihood of ever coming into play.

Myth #9: You Risk a Huge Tax Bill Should Your IUL Run out of Money Before You Die

As is often the case with IUL myths, this one has a kernel of truth but is shrouded in fallacy. First, let's parse out the truth. The IRS does require that any life insurance policy have at least $1 of cash value at the time of death, or it loses its tax-free protection. If the client violates this rule, they risk receiving a 1099 on all the gain in the cash value above and beyond their basis. This is our nightmare scenario, remember? Nobody wants to strategize their way into the 0% tax bracket in retirement only to get slapped with a huge tax bill due to a bankrupted IUL. For IUL policies whose growth accounts exceed their contributions (the vast majority of policies when structured properly), this poses a substantial risk.

Nobody is going to deny how disastrous this could be in theory, but in practice, there are several easy ways to ensure this never actually happens. First, as I mentioned in Myth #6, IULs should never be the only tax-free stream of income a client relies upon in retirement. As any good financial advisor will tell you, putting all of your eggs into one basket—regardless of which basket it is—is asking for disaster. Your IUL should always be perceived as a complement to multiple other tax-free sources of income (i.e., Roth IRAs, Roth 401(k)s, etc.).

If the IUL doesn't perform as expected over a period of time, simply lean on those other streams of tax-free income in the meantime. If the IUL is only one of multiple sources of tax-free income, the likelihood it could run out of money falls dramatically.

Second, as we saw in Chapter 6, some well-regarded IUL companies offer an over-loan protection rider that insulates you from the financial consequences of loaning yourself too much money. Should your cash value descend to dangerously low levels, companies can reduce your death benefit to the point where the remaining cash value pays up the policy, ensuring you won't receive that nasty 1099.

Third, this criticism is much more relevant to LIRPs that are tied to the stock market where combinations of market downturns and ill-managed distributions can send policies into a death spiral from which they may never recover, resulting in a taxable event (see Chapter 2). The IUL is different in a very fundamental way: while a stock-market based LIRP's cash value may be rapidly depleted in a down market, the IUL never gets credited worse than 0%. Certainly the cash value could reduce somewhat during a 0% crediting year due to ongoing insurance expenses, but given how well IULs have performed over the last 15 years of volatile market conditions, we shouldn't be overly concerned. In other words, while the risk is worth discussing, it isn't a compelling reason to forego the financial benefits of an IUL altogether.

Myth #10: Variable Loans Could Sink Your IUL Ship

Variable loans are a unique feature of IULs that can enhance distributions by allowing the loaned portion of the accumulation value to continue to receive index credits (say 7.5%). If the credit is consistently greater than the loan charge (say 5%), then the company is effectively paying you to take a policy loan. This additional credit (2.5% in this example) can further build cash value and increase the cumulative loans over the life of the policy.

Critics love to attack these types of arrangements because the client is responsible for the full brunt of loan costs (5% in this example) should the index suffer a down year and the client receive a 0% credit. And if, for example, you're faced with three years in a row of having to bear the full loan costs all while taking distributions, your accumulation value could fall dramatically.

What critics fail to consider is that some companies offer at least two different types of loans, the most common of which are variable loans *and* zero-cost loans. With the zero-cost loan, the amount being credited to the loan collateral account is the same as what's being charged. As we've seen in Chapters 4 and 7, some well-regarded companies even guarantee that these two numbers will never change, ensuring that distributions will always be tax-free *and* cost-free. Further, some companies allow you to "toggle" between these two types of loans every year, giving you an added measure of flexibility should you want to alter your strategy. So, if you take a variable loan in a down year, pay the full cost of the loan (5% in the above example) and don't want to risk paying those loan expenses two years in a row, you can always revert back to the zero-cost loan. Granted, not every IUL company offers this, but many do. All the more reason for you to do your research before choosing a life-long partner.

Finally, in order to fairly evaluate variable loans, we have to weigh the upside of the positive arbitrage in years where the index is up versus the downside risk of paying the loan costs when the index is down. To further explore this trade-off, let's take a look at the S&P 500 index over the last 70 years. Since the 1940s, the S&P 500 has been up an astounding 8 out of every 10 years. In two-thirds of those up years, the index has performed above and beyond many companies' caps (assuming an average cap of 13%). That means that over the last 70 years, you would have experienced a positive 8% arbitrage (assuming an average loan charge of 5% per year) over half the time! Conversely, you would have experienced the full brunt of the 5% loan charge in only 2 out every 10 years. For many clients who utilize the variable loan, this is a trade-off that's well worth making.

When utilized properly, a well-structured IUL can be a critical component of your tax-free retirement plan. In many cases, in fact, it can be impossible to get to the 0% tax bracket without it! However, financial gurus who are firmly entrenched in the tax-deferred paradigm (and who often times directly benefit from it), don't always see it that way. They often view the 0% tax bracket in retirement as an impossibility or even a pipe dream. As a result, tax-free alternatives such as the IUL get discounted, while their *perceived* deficiencies get enshrined on websites and blogs. These myths that financial gurus perpetuate are often riddled with half-truths and logical fallacies that give the IUL short shrift. When these myths are stripped of their biases and addressed openly and fairly, the IUL is revealed to be a welcome component to a thoughtful, well-balanced approach to tax-free retirement planning.

Chapter 7: Questions to Consider

1. How can you determine a realistic rate of return to expect on your IUL?

2. What are the circumstances that may cause an IUL cap rate to rise or fall?

3. In what scenarios might an insurance company revert to worst-case, guaranteed insurance expenses?

4. Why are death benefit guarantees incompatible with IUL loan distributions?

5. How can you protect yourself against the risks of taking an IUL loan in a flat market?

6. How can a retirement strategy that incorporates multiples streams of tax-free income protect you against the premature depletion of your IUL's cash value?

7. In what ways can you mitigate the potential risks of a variable loan?

CHAPTER EIGHT
A FINAL WORD

Considering all we've learned, there's no denying that choosing the right LIRP for you is akin to choosing the right spouse with whom to spend a lifetime. I am convinced that there is no better analogy for describing the process of finding the right LIRP. As with your potential mate, LIRPs have various qualities and quirks that need to align with your wants and needs, or else you run the risk of an unpleasant surprise—or even divorce—years into the marriage. For LIRPs to function optimally within your zero-tax retirement plan, they must possess a combination of attributes that you won't find through blind luck or casual investigation. Finding that ideal LIRP in a world where there are as many different LIRPs as there are cars on the road takes much more time and energy. And the process can be difficult to navigate if you haven't assembled a laundry list of qualities, a personalized standard if you will, by which to measure your various alternatives. Venturing onto the LIRP dating scene without a clearly defined list may lead to a hasty decision for which you may later pay a steep price. This is a process that must be undertaken seriously and soberly for much is at stake. If you take one thing away from this book, it's that you must "look before you LIRP!"

Having studied the different LIRP alternatives for the better part of my adult life, I am convinced that your search for the perfect LIRP, when properly undertaken, will lead to Indexed Universal Life. Simply put, the IUL is better equipped to get you to the 0% tax bracket in retirement than any other alternative. As an independent advisor who can offer the universe of LIRP alternatives to my clients, I consistently and repeatedly recommend the IUL. I don't have an axe to grind against the other choices. They have wonderful attributes and perform admirably in a variety of contexts. But I've evaluated the real and formidable pitfalls that stand between you and the 0% tax bracket in retirement and have concluded that only one specific alternative will allow you to safely circumnavigate them. Remember, *only* the IUL can offer *all* of the following qualities:

- Safe and Productive Growth
- Low Fees
- Tax-Free and Cost-Free Distributions
- A Long-Term Care Rider

Your LIRP may be lots of things, but if it lacks even one of these indispensable qualities, it is not ideally suited to get you into the 0% tax bracket in retirement. Something *will* go wrong along the way. I've witnessed dozens of instances where new clients couldn't figure out why their old LIRP wasn't performing as advertised. It wasn't because they had a bad product or had been misled by their prior advisor. Their LIRP simply was *not* designed to function as an integral part of a tax-free retirement strategy.

Remember, in many cases, it's impossible to get to the 0% tax bracket in retirement without the right LIRP. And if you just miss the 0% tax bracket because you have the wrong LIRP, the next best tax bracket isn't 1% or even 2%. It jumps all the way up to 10%! Throw in another 6% for state tax, and now you're at 16%. And if tax rates double, that 16% becomes 32%! Second place, in this instance, is hardly a consolation prize!

Here's my point: the stakes are incredibly high and it's important you get the LIRP right on your first try. What you don't know *can* hurt you! You don't want to get 10 years into your LIRP relationship and utter those fateful words, "What if?" *What if* you had opted for an LIRP that provided protection against a severe market downturn? *What if* you had properly evaluated your policy's fees and, in turn, its *real* rate of return? *What if* you had taken the time to understand the legalese that describes your loan provision? *What if* your LIRP had come with a long-term care rider that protected you against the single greatest risk you face in retirement? The time for uncovering skeletons and deal-breakers is now, before you enter into a long-term, legally binding contract!

But even after you decide that the IUL is the right LIRP with which to ride off into the sunset, your task is only partially complete. Just as not all LIRPs are created equal, neither are IULs. You must dig deeper, explore further, and determine conclusively that your IUL lives up to the qualities and attributes described in Chapter 6 of this book. Insist that your IUL have:

- A Guaranteed 0% Loan Provision (no worse than .25%)
- Capped Variable Loan Interest
- Interest in Arrears
- A Stable Cap Rate
- A Financially Stable Company
- An Over-Loan Protection Rider
- Daily or Weekly Sweeps

There are several IUL companies that bring these qualities to bear. The refining influence of the free market has led these companies to engineer their IULs to meet all of the above-described qualities. However, there are a number of companies who seem impervious to the advancements the free market promotes. They refuse to update their policies with the latest innovations that could transform their policies into lean, tax-free wealth building tools. Discerning between the good and the bad, however, is not always easy, so you must be vigilant! I repeat, you must "look before your LIRP!" The type of investigation and research you must undertake does take extra effort, but trust me, it could save you a world of pain and heartache down the road.

Now that you've educated yourself, take the next step by discussing this book with the advisor who shared it with you. Insist on an IUL that conforms to the gold standards set forth in these pages. Remember, good is the enemy of best and the devil is *always* in the details—never more so than with the IUL. If the trusted advisor that gave you this book answers all your questions to your satisfaction, then it is likely you have found an LIRP candidate with which you can engage in a long-term commitment. At long last, you have found your LIRP soulmate! You have successfully set the stage for a fruitful, rewarding and long-lasting LIRP marriage. Congratulations and best of luck as you begin your journey towards the 0% tax bracket.

For bulk discounts and CDs, go to

thepowerofzerobook.com

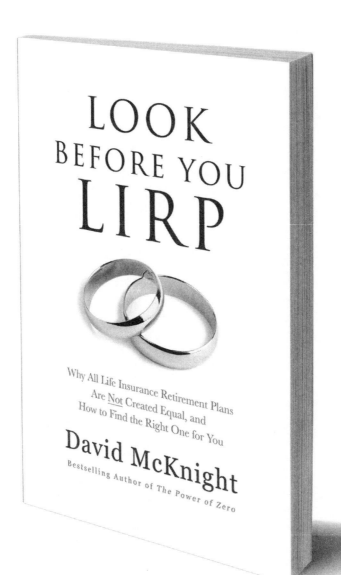

LOOK
BEFORE YOU
LIRP

Why All Life Insurance Retirement Plans
Are Not Created Equal, and
How to Find the Right One for You

David McKnight

Bestselling Author of The Power of Zero

For bulk discounts and CDs, go to
lookbeforeyoulirp.com